"This book is nothing short of extra[ordinary] ... have *ever* had words on a page meet me ... where I am. For every single one of us who has been knocked to the floor these last few years, *The Gift of the Unexpected* offers us a way forward: by first going back. And this time truly leaning into the transformation offered. Jillian's words are equal parts raw, real, and redemptive. I can't wait to share this beautiful book with everyone I know!"

> Mary Marantz, bestselling author of *Dirt* and *Slow Growth Equals Strong Roots*, host of *The Mary Marantz Show*

"Intense. Stunning. Needed. Jillian's words will help you discover beauty in the unexpected."

> Leslie Means, creator of Her View From Home

"This book extends an invitation to see that what cracks our hearts can also expand them. Thoughtful and honest, Jillian's story of transformation reminds us that God is present and pursuing us, even in the most unexpected moments of our lives. Read and be changed."

> Kayla Craig, author of *To Light Their Way* and creator of Liturgies for Parents

"In *The Gift of the Unexpected*, Jillian reveals the beauty of transformation through life's difficult circumstances when we choose to *undergo* rather than *overcome* our hardships. This subtle shift points toward hope in the middle of life's inevitable unexpected moments and will leave you forever changed."

> Mikala Albertson, MD; author of *Ordinary on Purpose: Surrendering Perfect and Discovering Beauty Amid the Rubble*

"Written with gentleness, thoughtfulness, and honesty, Jillian Benfield's particular story of giving birth to a child with Down syndrome is a balm for all of us who dare to doubt and dare to hope that God is present in the midst of the unexpected hardships and unexpected beauty of our lives."

Amy Julia Becker, author of *To Be Made Well*
and *A Good and Perfect Gift*

"Jillian's story reminds us that no matter how painful, the unexpected circumstances of our life aren't the end of our story. God can take what shakes up our world and turn it into our deepest purpose. Jillian's words are beautifully raw and will meet anyone who's suffering with validation and hope."

Kelli Bachara, licensed professional clinical
counselor and writer

"In *The Gift of the Unexpected*, Jillian Benfield shows us that life's unexpected—and unwanted—twists and turns can lead us toward purpose and reveal both the power and significance of landing in unanticipated circumstances. Benfield takes us on a journey of hurting, healing, hoping, and ultimately becoming."

Jenny Albers, author of *Courageously Expecting: 30 Days
of Encouragement for Pregnancy After Loss*

"An essential read for anyone who's ever faced unmet expectations. Jillian tackles the complex realities of life in a way that puts God's purpose into perspective. Her stories are authentic and practical as she gently reminds us it's okay to not be okay."

Allen Thomas, lead pastor, Outer West Community Church

The
Gift
of the
Unexpected

The
Gift
of the
Unexpected

DISCOVERING WHO YOU WERE MEANT
TO BE WHEN LIFE GOES OFF PLAN

JILLIAN BENFIELD

BETHANYHOUSE
a division of Baker Publishing Group
Minneapolis, Minnesota

© 2023 by Jillian Benfield

Published by Bethany House Publishers
Minneapolis, Minnesota
www.bethanyhouse.com

Bethany House Publishers is a division of
Baker Publishing Group, Grand Rapids, Michigan

Printed in the United States of America

Library of Congress Cataloging-in-Publication Control Number: 2022040928
Names: Benfield, Jillian, author.
Title: The gift of the unexpected : discovering who you were meant to be when life goes off plan / Jillian Benfield.
Description: Minneapolis, Minnesota : Bethany House, a division of Baker Publishing Group, [2023] | Includes bibliographical references.
Identifiers: LCCN 2022040928 | ISBN 9780764240492 (paperback) | ISBN 9780764241604 (casebound) | ISBN 9781493440818 (ebook)
Subjects: LCSH: Resilience (Personality trait)—Religious aspects—Christianity. | Hope—Religious aspects—Christianity. | Christian life.
Classification: LCC BV4597.58.R47 B45 2023 | DDC 248.8/6--dc23/eng/20221223
LC record available at https://lccn.loc.gov/2022040928

Scripture quotations are from THE HOLY BIBLE, NEW INTERNATIONAL VERSION®, NIV® Copyright © 1973, 1978, 1984, 2011 by Biblica, Inc.® Used by permission. All rights reserved worldwide.

Cover design by Studio Gearbox

The author is represented by Illuminate Literary Agency, www.illuminateliterary.com.

23   24   25   26   27   28   29   8   7   6   5   4   3   2

To Andy

Thank you for loving who I was before the unexpected,
who I was during, and who I am now becoming.

Contents

Introduction

The Gift of Before-and-After

My life fell apart with a twenty-second phone call. The words on the other end of the line took the air from my lungs. My cheeks instantly became wet, and my legs went weak.

Some events are so momentous that they erect a divide in the timeline of our lives. There is a glimpse of time that ends life as we know it and begins a whole new one. It's called the before-and-after moment.

My before-and-after moment came when I was twenty-seven years old and pregnant with my second child. I could never go back to the time before those words were spoken. Life would never be the same. *I* would never be the same.

The words came from my husband, Andy. "The doctor called me, and it's . . . um . . . it's not good. I'm coming home."

My heavy, twenty-two-weeks pregnant body slid onto the cold kitchen-floor tiles of our new rental house, many of our belongings still unpacked. I dropped my phone and frantically cried, "Oh no, oh no, oh no. This doesn't feel real, this doesn't feel real, this doesn't feel real." It was as if my mouth had to repeat what my head and heart didn't want to be true.

Years ago, if you had told me I would one day write a book about how this moment was in reality the greatest gift of my life, I wouldn't have believed you. But I have done just that, because my before-and-after moment led to both the unbecoming and the becoming of me.

I believe your unexpected moment, your unexpected life, holds the same potential for you. But only if you resist society's insistence on *overcoming* the unexpected and choose instead to *undergo* it.

Do a quick Google Images search of the word *overcoming*, and you will see people standing atop mountains, hands raised over their heads in a stance that claims victory. Now search *undergoing*, and you will find people about to be cut open by surgeons. The healing they need can be found only by digging deep into the dark spaces within. The newness comes only by confronting the pain. And we know it's not over when the patient awakes. The patient will have to pursue recovery.

Yes, the undergoing I'm suggesting is like that.

A synonym for the word *overcome* is *suppress*. This is the message we so often get from our Western and church cultures. We are expected to go from positive to positive. We're expected to be the PR team for Jesus and ourselves by feeling our pain for the shortest amount of time possible. We're expected to push through the sadness and grief and to bring our #goodvibesonly. We're expected to return to our normal selves as quickly as we can.

That's the mark of the strong, we're told.

And to be honest, it's probably easier now than ever to overcome our unexpected circumstances. We push through by stuffing our feelings down and numbing out with Netflix, social media, and wine that can be delivered to our doorstep. And we may just accomplish what we set out to do. We may just get to that metaphorical mountaintop and show the world how strong we are because we have overcome the sadness, we have come out on the other side of grief intact despite our crushing experience.

But if we do this, we come out on the other side wrapped in sameness. We miss out on the opportunity to be transformed.

The real mark of strength is when we do the difficult and slow work of walking through the dark place where we find ourselves. We must sit with the hurt and confusion instead of suppressing them, but then we must allow them to be our guide. We must listen to the voices while in the depths—the voice of God, the whispers of our own hearts, and the input of others who have also spent time below. That's because listening is essential to receiving the grace necessary for transformation.[1]

If we are brave enough to take in our present surroundings and eventually work through them, God can use our unexpected circumstances to help us first rediscover our core selves. He does this by helping us tear down the false constructs we've built atop our identities. If we let Him, He will show us what parts of ourselves we've added that need to go, what parts need to stay, and what we need to acquire. And when the dust has settled from the demolition, we'll begin to see ourselves more clearly as wholly His and wholly beloved.

Only when we start to see ourselves as our creator always has will He remind us that all new life begins in the darkness. Just as He formed us in the depths of the womb, He can shape us once more in this unexpected place. By feeling our pain instead of ignoring it, we can connect to the aching of the world from which we were perhaps once distanced. Through this work, then, we become more whole and more real than we were before. We not only find our healing but begin to see how God wants us to bring this healing to the world.

That's when we take first steps out of the darkness and toward that mountain peak. We take them in the same skin we wore when the unexpected first hit our lives but with a new-ness running through our veins. The unexpected pain may have broken our hearts for a time, but with time, we are broken wide open to possibilities anew, possibilities greater than ourselves. And when we get to the summit, I don't think the snapshot of us will show our hands raised in victory, believing we've made it. Instead, our faces will be pointed toward the sun, knowing this is only the start of a new beginning.

This is when we ask God to show us the way forward. This is when we ask Him to set this good transformation to purpose—purposes beyond the confines of our individual lives. This is when we climb back down the mountain and start participating in this life we get to live in a whole new way. This is when we have fully realized the gift that can come from the unexpected—ourselves made new.

Let me stop right here—not for the last time—to say you don't have to classify your unexpected circumstances as good. As you will see, I was misinformed about my before-and-after moment. But I have had other unexpected moments as well—open-heart surgery for my older son, a miscarriage, and then a fetal intervention surgery and a horrific medical injury for my youngest child. I do not consider these events to be good.

But what I have experienced is this: God can make good come from the unexpected heartaches we experience in this life. And most of the time, that good is a change from within.

I originally started writing this book trying to answer a question: Was my life always meant to end up this way? I was searching for the God of certainty and instead found the God of surprise. He surprises us with the beauty of the unex-pected and the grace He provides when the unexpected is anything but. Through the years—and through many unexpected events—I've discovered that God does not promise us a steady life; He promises resurrection. He said we will have trouble in this world but to take heart because He has overcome the world.[2]

This promise is not just about the grand finale of our lives when we take our last breath and catch our first glimpse of heaven. It's also about the many resurrections we will experience in the here and now. This vow of God is intertwined with all our unexpected endings and beginnings, because it is often through the unexpected that our creator shows us who we are and points us to who He wants us to become.

Maybe your before-and-after experience left a gaping hole in your life, and you just can't imagine anything good down there. I can't tell you this hole will be filled the same way it once was, but if you are willing to take this journey, if you are willing to walk back past the point before everything fell apart so you can move forward changed, something good can come from this. We are known and loved by a God who gives beauty where our deepest, unexpected hurts once resided.

And He often does this through the work of transformation.

When you experienced your before-and-after moment, did you notice that your world came to a screeching halt but somehow everyone else's kept turning? And turning. And turning. And turning.

I did.

When Andy called, the doctor had just let him know the blood screen on our unborn son had come back positive for a genetic anomaly. But we didn't know which one, and we needed to return to the man's office to find out.

My mom was driving Andy and me through the winding back road to the hospital when we passed a group of young boys riding scooters and laughing as though all was right in the world. Their happiness highlighted my despair. I stared ahead, dazed, wondering how this could be.

For you, maybe it was getting the dreaded medical results at your desk while coworkers laughed and chatted away. Or learning of your spouse's betrayal and only seconds later hearing your baby scream because she needed to be fed. Or perhaps you were walking to your car after saying goodbye to a loved one for the final time when parents strolled by holding new life, filled to the brim with possibilities.

When others' lives carry on with the usual threads and weave in new ones but your life is suddenly barren, it can pierce your soul. Your threads are now frayed, and you're left unable to fathom how it can all possibly be. But having been through my moment when time paused and hung and ached, I've come to believe that the world that keeps cruelly spinning is God's way of pointing us to hope. I have ultimately learned that the unexpected can lead us from the depths of desolation to a resurrected self, a resurrected way of living God has called us to.

Chatting coworkers can act as a reminder that we will one day again hum along with life. A hungry baby can remind us that, although empty now, we will one day be full again. And the loss of a loved one will always hurt, but a couple high on possibilities can remind us that one day we will dream anew.

First sunset, then sunrise. First storm, then a rainbow. First death, then resurrection. That's what they say. But, of course, it doesn't happen just like that. We experience hours of inconceivable darkness, strong winds that threaten to knock us down, and the hopelessness of an unopened tomb.

Yet right there in the midst of it, God is making something new.

This book is about inviting Him to make something new in us when the unexpected leaves our lives and ourselves unrecognizable. Because after we've done our time processing, grieving, and lamenting, life begins to stir. The dawn breaks, the clouds fade, and the stone rolls away. Yes, life moves on, and one day, so will we. But hopefully, we will take steps toward a life different from when we started.

The unexpected can lead us from the depths of desolation to a resurrected self, a resurrected way of living God has called us to.

This new and different life is the gift of the unexpected, and I've written this book for those willing to unwrap it. But it's like one of those super-sized packages at kids' birthday parties, where the giver wrapped it in layers of paper for the receiver to remove before finally reaching the prize. This gift requires our time, effort, and patience. What we find inside is not our old life, our old faith, our old perspective but ourselves, wholly loved and wholly transformed.

The Gift of the Unexpected is divided into three parts.

In Part 1, we'll see how to do the work of returning to ourselves and seeing ourselves as our creator sees us—beloved not because of what we do or don't do but because of who we are.

In Part 2, we'll see that once we know ourselves, we're primed for change, for transformation. But before we get there, we must feel our pain so we can get in touch with our humanity, stop distancing ourselves from the hurt of the world, and instead, allow it to work in us and through us.

17

And in Part 3, we'll see that if we do the work of internal transformation, spurred on by our unexpected circumstances, we can discover who God wants us to become.

Each chapter, then, is divided into three sections. The first is where I tell you my unexpected story in hopes you will see yourself and your own story there.

The second is titled The Gift. Here, I lean on Scripture, research, and metaphor to draw out the lessons I've learned from the unexpected along the way. It's important to note that I was not learning these lessons in the first few chapters, the chapters where I'm wrecked with grief. They came with time, prayer, reading, good counsel, reflection—and ultimately, undergoing.

And finally, under the heading The Gift of You, I provide journaling questions to help you reflect on who you were during the heat of the unexpected, who you are now in regard to the topic of the chapter, and who you want to become in light of these unexpected lessons. You will also find journaling space to dig deep and discover the gift of the unexpected—discovering who you were meant to be.

God will set our unexpected transformations to purpose but only if we are willing to participate.

This path of the unexpected life is steep, twisty, and at times lovely. And although the road is long and some points are scary, we arrive at overlooks now and again, where the views are extraordinary. But we must walk it. We must be bold enough to face our realities both past and present to get to the place where God wants us to arrive. And when we get there, to our new beginning, we can't help but also look back to see how He made our lives over again from dust, one more time.

Dear reader, you will see me say that my grief about my unexpected moment was based on ignorance. It was based on my faulty beliefs of what constitutes a good and worthy life. Nevertheless, the subsequent grief was real.

You see, the twenty-second phone call that knocked me to the floor did break my life apart. I just didn't realize how God would use those pieces. He pulled most of them back, swept some away, and added new ones. The result has been an evolving picture that has more beauty and depth than I could have ever imagined.

The unexpected gave me my son Anderson.

And in doing so, it also gave me, me.

Let's begin unwrapping to discover the gift that awaits you— that through the unexpected you can become who God always imagined you to be.

Part 1

The Gift of Returning to Yourself

Owning our story and loving ourselves through that
process is the bravest thing that we will ever do.

—Brené Brown, *The Gifts of Imperfection*

1

Breaking Open

Many of the happiest moments of my life run together in a brightly colored blur.

I remember the delight I felt when, surprised, I walked up to a white blanket, pink roses, and Andy down on one knee waiting for me. But I don't recall his exact words when he asked me to marry him. I remember sitting in my white gown, overjoyed and even giddy while laughing at my dad's toast during our wedding reception. But I can't recall the content. I remember the ecstasy-riddled joy I felt just after seeing our first child's fresh pink skin for the first time. But I don't recall the words Andy and I spoke to each other as Violet lay on my chest after delivery.

But when I look back at my worst moments, I'm haunted by the smallest details.

The years 2013 and 2014 had already been laced with the unexpected. Andy graduated dental school on an air force scholarship, and soon after he moved his tassel, the military sent us from Augusta, Georgia, to Las Vegas, Nevada, for a one-year residency program. Then after spending hours toiling over what to put on our "dream sheet," a list of our preferred locations for our next assignment, we opened an envelope with orders to a location that felt more like a nightmare—Alamogordo, New Mexico.

Alamogordo is where they tested the first atomic bomb in 1945, and this news felt like a bomb of our own had gone off, blowing up the scripts we'd written in our heads for what the near future would look like. Particularly for me. Moving to Alamogordo meant no chance of going back to my career as a TV journalist.

We had no idea the plot was about to become so twisted that we wouldn't even recognize the story as our own. We would think this was the kind of narrative that belonged to other people, not us. Although now I'm so grateful our stories played out the way they have, at the time I couldn't see how anything good could come from these unscripted parts of our lives.

Thankfully, I was wrong. Thankfully, this was the beginning of unlearning and learning, of breaking and stretching, of changing and transforming.

Eight days after we arrived in our new and remote town, I was twenty weeks pregnant with our second child and in the waiting room at a new OB-GYN's office for my anatomy scan. The ultrasound technician greeted Andy and me and escorted us to her examination room. She had short sun-kissed hair and skin to match, and there was something gentle about her that I liked right away.

She asked me to pull up my silky top. I took a deep breath, my chest expanded against my skin, and for the first time in weeks I felt centered. In the chaos of moving, in the disappointment about where we'd landed, I had nearly forgotten I was carrying a miracle inside me.

24

She took her white squeeze bottle out of its holster and covered my midsection with warm aquamarine goo, then untangled her wand to show us a glimpse of our future. Another baby.

"It's a boy!" she concluded almost immediately..

Andy cried happy tears. I cried too. And for a few minutes, everything was perfect. In our young married years, we'd daydreamed about our future family. We'd picked out names for both sons and daughters yet to be, and now the dream was becoming reality. Our family portrait would be what we wanted it to be.

As I stared at the smooth white ceiling above, pondering the nuances of a brother-sister relationship between children less than two years apart, I didn't realize how much time had passed. The technician had me turn on my side to get the last measurement, and when she got it, she thanked us, flipped on the lights, and walked out the door.

A cheery nurse bounced into our room minutes later and said, "Well, the doctor isn't here, so everything must look great!" But as soon as she'd said those words, he walked in wearing the traditional white coat—and a concerned look on his face.

"We need to discuss some things on the ultrasound," he said.

He pulled up the screen and pointed to the black and white image. "You see here a bright spot on the baby's heart. The heart appears to be working fine, but this spot can sometimes indicate other things may be wrong."

He continued to tell us our baby also had a thickened nuchal fold, a fold of skin at the back of the neck. The measurement was only slightly off but still enlarged. He explained that with those two markers, our baby had an increased chance of having one of the more-common trisomies—13, 18, or 21.

"What does that mean?" I asked.

"It means your baby could have a genetic condition like Down syndrome."

The room grew blurry, and my back broke out in fire as the doctor's voice began sounding like one of the monotone adults in the animated versions of *Peanuts*. I couldn't concentrate on what he was saying, because the thought *I can't be a special needs mom, I can't be a special needs mom* played in my head over and over again like a skipping CD.*

The doctor explained that a new blood test was on the market, and we would have the results in about two weeks. The scene was still blurry and began to spin, but somehow, with Andy's help, I managed to walk to the lab.

They took my blood.

And then we waited.

Waiting admits a lack of control. The situation was out of our hands. Yet as we waited for the blood test results, we tried to grab the power in a powerless fight. We told ourselves a "Podunk" Alamogordo hospital probably didn't have the best technology and booked an ultrasound appointment in El Paso, the largest nearby city.

Once again, I lifted my shirt, but this time I shuddered as the new ultrasound technician squeezed the familiar blue goo across my midsection. And then, there he was again. Our son. Dressed in black and white. His spine wiggled, and his hands stretched across the nice office's big projection screen. I wanted to love him, but now I was afraid of falling.

She measured his nuchal fold and looked at his heart. "This baby is completely normal," she concluded.

Normal.

*Dear reader, this is the only time you'll see me use the term *special needs*. From the disability community, I've learned that the word *disability* is preferred. But in this case, I want you to know the very real thoughts I had in this moment.

When I was a senior in high school, my parents sat me down in a New York City restaurant while we were on vacation, some cozy little spot in Little Italy.

"Jill, if you want to do this, we'll support you," my mom said.

My parents were offering to move me to the city to pursue a Broadway musical career instead of a journalism degree, but I dismissed the idea immediately. I wanted the wild and free college experience. I wanted the big football school and frat parties. I also knew my parents had a bloated confidence in my talents. Maybe I had the singing voice, but I couldn't dance and could barely act. It would take a lot of classes to get me there, and I wasn't sure if I had "it" anyway.

But really, that type of move was too out there for me, too risky. I wanted just a notch above normal, and a TV journalism career would be the perfect mix of flashy and practical.

Now normal sounded extremely appealing. But with only a six-day gap between ultrasounds, how could the results be so different? Like a pendulum, I swung into times of self-affirmed peace and just as quickly into doubt.

I remember when the pendulum stopped swinging. A storm brewed above the mountain behind our home. The eight more days of waiting for the blood test results had started to bubble up my emotions, and I was about to burst. My mom, who'd come from Florida to help us unpack, and I were sitting on the porch when tears of frustration and fear started trickling down my cheeks.

"All day long I've felt like he does have something," I choked out.

There was a slight pause, as my mom didn't know what to say. Who would? But then she suddenly spoke, pointing. "Look! As soon as you said that, a rainbow appeared."

I turned around to peer at the colorful view in the still-cloudy sky, then hung my head. "I don't think that's a good sign."

I thought God was telling me He was still there—but I wouldn't get the news I wanted.

The next day Andy came home for lunch in a good mood. He liked his new dental clinic, and my ever-optimistic husband believed we would get good news about the blood test that day and this ordeal would be over. I hid my doubts as I kissed him goodbye and handed him his hat. He went back to work.

I was still cleaning up from lunch when my phone rang. It was Andy.

"The doctor called me, and it's . . . um . . . it's not good. I'm coming home."

I dropped the phone, and that's when my twenty-two-weeks-pregnant body fell to the cold tiled floor. My mom held my head as hot, sticky tears poured down my face. "I'm so sorry, I'm so sorry," she cried.

We sat there on the kitchen floor, bodies entangled the way they had when I was a child with a skinned knee or a teenager with a bruised heart. And we stayed in that pool of each other's shock until Andy walked in.

I had never seen the look he wore on his face; the light he normally radiates was out. I followed him into our bedroom, where we lay on our yellow duvet, held each other, and cried. I'd chosen the yellow Pottery Barn cover when we registered for our new life together. It was happy. It was perfect. I didn't know our story would turn into a sad one, the cover now damp with a pain we couldn't exchange.

Andy ran to the bathroom and started vomiting. I ran my hands up and down his back as his body rejected the shock. When he finished, I unbuttoned his constricting military uniform. He rested his head on my enlarged chest, and his warm tears fell down my shirt and onto my round belly. We had just turned twenty-seven years old, and when I got pregnant, there was only a one in thousand chance we would conceive a child with a trisomy. We were on the wrong side of the statistics.

Or so we thought.

I remember everything.

An hour later, I walked into my new OB-GYN's office for the second time but now in a dreamlike state. Only the objects directly in front of me felt real—feet walking, backsides in chairs, magazines on tables. Everything else was hazy.

"Benfield?"

"Benfield?"

I snapped out of it, and then Andy did too. We moved to the front desk, where we found the receptionist and another front-office employee with heavy eyes.

It was clear everyone who worked there knew, but what did they know? Was it trisomy 13—fatal, trisomy 18—sometimes fatal, or trisomy 21 (Down syndrome)—livable? I didn't want any of them. I wanted a way out.

In the hall connecting the waiting and exam rooms, I felt as if I were walking the green mile, certain our fate, in one way or another, was death.

Now I wish I would have known this moment was instead an invitation to a new life.

Everyone else knew of the execution about to take place, and I kept my eyes down to avoid the looks from the gallery. I was the twenty-seven-year-old with the body that failed, a body I could barely lift onto the exam table covered in white crinkled paper. Andy and I waited under the fluorescent lights in silence. There was nothing left to say until our fate was known.

The doctor finally walked in and cut through the sterile quiet. "Well, it's not good. Your baby has a 99 percent chance of having Down syndrome."

After riddling us with his opinions about Down syndrome, he followed up with, "But don't worry. You don't have to be heroes. If you decide to go through with the pregnancy, you can have the baby here. We can keep him comfortable, but we don't have to do anything drastic to prolong his life."

In other words, we could let our son die of natural causes.

We walked out, and the heavy-eyed receptionist handed me an envelope with information about a Down syndrome support group more than an hour away.

I didn't want support. I wanted to disappear. I wanted a baby whose life wasn't over before it began.

This is where I should tell you this level of honesty is grueling, but I want you to know the depth of my story. I want you to know how little I knew then and how I feel so differently now.

There *was* a death that day—just not the death I thought.

The details of the day are sharp. I remember the bushiness of the doctor's furrowed brows and the weakness of his mouth. I remember the horror I felt at his words and the guilt I felt over my emotions. I remember the drive home and the afternoon light shining too brightly, and my craving its absence.

But I have no details of the night. I only know it was as dark as my memory.

~~~~~~~

Two days later I found myself looking for armor inside my closet.

Our new town was so remote that a maternal-fetal medicine specialist and her team traveled there only once a month, but we got an appointment. And because of our positive screen for Down syndrome, we were her first of the day.

What will make me look like my life isn't falling apart while also conveying to this doctor who cares for high-risk pregnancies that I need her to be gentle?

After choosing a white peasant, wholesome-looking maternity top, I stared at myself in the bathroom mirror, then at the cross necklace Andy gifted me after Violet's birth. It was lying on the counter, staring back at me, revealing me.

Do I wear it?

I didn't want to. If Jesus made the blind see and the deaf hear, why wouldn't He heal my son of this lifelong diagnosis? It wasn't a matter of whether He could; it was a question of why He had not.

I thought wearing the cross close to my heart might help get rid of the ugliness lurking in its chambers. I thought it might help remove any unspoken desires to hit the rewind button, to get my old life back. I reluctantly fastened the white-gold clasp around my neck, then looked up at my reflection again.

The shiny cross had the same effect on me as it always does—hope. I felt a small surge of the feeling that had gone missing ever since military orders had forced us out of our exciting Las Vegas home to this barren New Mexico town only weeks earlier.

My hope was that God would still come through for me and for my son, in the way I prescribed.

Andy and I walked into the doctor's small waiting room. The bottom halves of its walls were covered with vinyl wood-look planks, the top with a stained white plaster. There was a hum in the air, from what I don't know. Maybe an overworked air conditioner. Photos of newborns adorned in nothing but handstitched hats lined the entire lobby.

My heart sank. *No one will want a photo of my baby.*

I wondered if Andy was thinking the same thing.

A woman just a few years older than me sat across from us. Her pale hair was glued to her head with an unkempt bun perched on top. Her stark black glasses frames didn't match her worn purple T-shirt. She wore no armor, which was perplexing to me. *She must be pregnant with twins*, I thought. No one could possibly be experiencing the depth of the tragedy that landed my legging-clad backside in that waiting room chair.

Grief whispers lies of isolation again and again.

We eventually walked back to a tiny exam room, where the doctor greeted us. She was an older woman with a tiny frame, a blunt haircut, and a no-nonsense demeanor. I liked that. I couldn't handle the weight of anyone's empathy without crumbling.

She looked at me directly. "You can pretty much take the blood screen results to the bank, but if I were your sister, I'd tell you to have an amniocentesis."

So I did.

I wanted to know for sure, and in those raw first days, my fear of losing my baby wasn't as great as my fear of raising him. She performed another ultrasound on my weary abdomen to find the safest point of entry, and guilt washed over me as I looked at my son's unsuspecting frame wiggle on the black and white screen. Then she told me to count to three.

"One . . . two . . . three."

She stuck a large needle into my womb to extract fluid, which would give us a clear answer—forty-six chromosomes or an extra forty-seventh. But she had trouble getting enough fluid for the test. My body didn't want to let go, making the procedure last longer than it should. Yet the pain of why she was doing it hurt worse than the sting and pressure.

A tear rolled down my face as the sign of Jesus frantically moved up and down on my chest.

Forsaken.

A distant relative gave us a large clock engraved with "BEN-FIELDS, EST. 2009" as a wedding gift. I remember hearing it *tick, tick, tick* when I was a weekend news anchor and home alone on Thursdays and Fridays while Andy was at dental school. I tried to keep myself busy. I volunteered, did housework, and cooked, but when I got lonely with too little to do, I would hear that *tick, tick, tick.*

Life got louder once Andy graduated, he entered active-duty military service, and our first baby arrived. The quiet I once knew was now filled with little cries and lullabies. I hadn't heard the clock ticking since Violet was born a year and a half earlier. But now as September began to fade and signs of fall appeared, I heard it again.

Tick, tick, tick.

The specialist told us it would take ten to fourteen days to get the amniocentesis results. As we left her office, we let ourselves feel hopeful that our baby would be the exception, the previous test a false positive. The first few days of the waiting process were easy, some even joyful. Then the tenth day came . . .

Tick, tick, tick.

Attempting to fill the spaces between the minute and second hands, I left the house with Violet in the morning and tried to get to know our new little town. I even experienced five-minute periods when I forgot I was waiting for the biggest news of my life.

But in the afternoons, when I knew the lunch break at the doctor's office was over, it would hit me again. I held my phone with sweaty palms and a weak stomach and stared at the screen. Anytime it made a noise, I felt like vomiting. I spent those afternoons thinking, *Just a few more hours and then I'm safe for the day.*

We'd instructed the doctor to call Andy since he's more medical-minded than I am, and if I never left my phone, then I couldn't be caught off guard by his name appearing on the screen. I wouldn't be knocked down to the floor again. Only, no amount of preparation can soften the news of what is life-altering and permanent. It is always unexpected, even when the evidence hints at its coming.

Neither could I have known the transformation God sets into motion when life as we know it ends—and then a new one begins.

Tick, tick, tick.

Late on a Thursday, I was changing Violet's diaper when Andy called. I held her steady with one hand and hit the speaker button with the other. Because it was so late in the day, it didn't occur to me this was *the* call.

"The doctor called me with the results. He has Down syndrome."

The clock stopped. I was no longer threatened by the *tick, tick, tick.* The dreaded moment had passed.

After I hung up, I finished changing Violet's diaper and yelled to my mom in the other room, "Results are in, and he has Down syndrome," as casually as if I were yelling, "Hey, what do you want for dinner tonight?"

I sat on the floor to play with my daughter, and my mom walked into the room. She put her arm around me, squeezed my shoulder . . . and nothing. I had no reaction. No tears. No emotions.

I was numb.

Andy and I had been in a roll-over car crash a couple of years prior, and we survived the impact with no obvious signs of trauma. We had no cuts, no broken bones. The sheriff of Jackson County, Georgia, drove us to our North Augusta home, and we rode stunned and silent but unharmed. Not until I started undressing to take a shower did I realize I had wet myself.

The impact of the crash slowly started revealing itself, first with hurt backs, next with physical therapy appointments and a new car to buy.

The effects of this new impact were also slow to appear. I rode passenger through the moments after, aware of life happening around me but replaying the crash in my mind as the scenery passed by.

It started with a steady flow of wordless tears more than an hour after getting the news. I cried over my mom's homemade lasagna while still managing to eat it—because pregnancy. I tried to talk it out with Andy on the porch in the shadow of our desert mountain view, fluctuating between anger and sadness. But he wasn't giving me the grand reaction I wanted. It wasn't enough. I needed to feel the full weight of this definitive truth. I needed to remove the armored clothes and put on a sackcloth like they did in ancient times.

I undressed, then folded a thick towel and placed it on the shower floor. I turned on the hot water, sat my backside on the towel, and let my fate wash over me. The beads pelted me with the realization of how quickly our lives had changed forever. The clock would never turn back. Our lives would never return to what they once were.

The cry I cried on the shower floor wasn't an ugly cry; it was a scary wail. I had witnessed the sound that came out of my body only a few times before, back when I was a journalist and drove up to a tragic scene too early.

It's the cry that only comes from sudden loss. Because that's what I *believed* it was. I used to be a witness to tragedy. Now I *was* the tragedy.

When I was a reporter and sat across from victims I interviewed, it felt as if an invisible barrier separated me from them. Because of my position, my financial security, my privilege, I was safe. They were on the side of the misfortune; I was protected, set apart. I guess in one way or another, we tell ourselves these lies to keep living. We search for reasons why his car crashed or why her body got cancer. We put the blame on the blameless to hide from our own fragility.

As I curled up naked, cradling the boy who was making me question, making me feel, and unknowingly making me, *me*, I was aware of how exposed I had always been. I was just pretending before.

The water finally turned cold, the tears and my skin dried, and I got my awkward pregnant body off the shower floor and went to bed empty.

——— **The Gift** ———

Dear reader, in the introduction to this book, you saw me say my grief about my son's Down syndrome diagnosis was based on my ignorance. And particularly around my ignorance about disability. It was based on fear and my unknowing ableism.* On my bad assumptions about God, myself, and the world.

No matter the reason for my grief, however, it was real. And that's where I want to meet you, now, in your real grief.

*Disability activist Leah Smith defines ableism this way: "Ableism is a set of beliefs or practices that devalue and discriminate against people with physical, intellectual, or psychiatric disabilities and often rests on the assumption that disabled people need to be 'fixed' in one form or the other." Center for Disability Rights – Integration, Independence, Civil Rights, cdrnys.org/blog/uncategorized/ableism.

The late singer Nightbirde rose to quick fame in 2021 after she wowed the judges of *America's Got Talent* with her beautiful voice and painful story. At the time of the performance, her cancer diagnosis gave her a 2 percent chance of survival.

She penned this on her blog: "I have heard it said that some people can't see God because they won't look low enough, and it's true. If you can't see him, look lower. God is on the bathroom floor."[1]

I know this because I met Him there.

I know this because He helped me meet myself there.

Whether your unexpected sorrow is attached to something you will feel differently about one day or is tethered to what can only be classified as a tragedy, I want to meet you on your bathroom floor, where God is so very present.

I want to tell you that your willingness to feel all you need to feel here on these cold tiles is necessary. I want to come and sit cross-legged next to you, stare into your damp eyes, and tell you to let yourself break apart because that is necessary to breaking open.

Researcher and author Dr. Brené Brown studies shame, and she defines it as an "intensely painful feeling or experience of believing that we are flawed and therefore unworthy of love and belonging."[2] We experience shame when we believe we've done something or failed to do something that could make us lose our connections to others—love—or perhaps something that makes us feel unworthy of having connection in the first place.

To deepen her study around shame, Dr. Brown interviewed more than twelve hundred participants who were living what she called "wholehearted" lives. Every one of us experiences shame, yet these people believe and live as though they are enough.

What emerged as a key category in both her study on shame and in her study on wholeheartedness was vulnerability.[3]

In her book *Braving the Wilderness*, Dr. Brown writes this about vulnerability: "Our families and culture believed that the vulnerability that it takes to acknowledge pain was weakness, so we were taught anger, rage, and denial instead. But what we know now is that when we deny our emotion, it owns us. When we own our emotion, we can rebuild and find our way through the pain."[4]

Vulnerability is not weakness. It takes tremendous amounts of courage to be vulnerable with others and even to ourselves on the bathroom floor. Vulnerability is required to build resilience to shame. Vulnerability is required for us to live wholeheartedly as ourselves.

You see, who I was on the shower floor that night was someone who had let the world tell her who she was. Somewhere along the way, I'd absorbed the message that my worthiness came from my ability to perform. That was my armor. If I could just outperform the person next to me, if I could make it look like my life was perfect, if I always looked my best, then I would be worthy of connection and praise.

I hid behind this armor. I was not vulnerable. I lived scared.

I wonder what lies that lay heavy across your shoulders you absorbed while the water pelted you with your new reality—and maybe even still. Did they say you were too much? Did they say you weren't enough? Did they say you were incapable of taking risks? Did they say you would never break the cycle of addiction or abuse? Did they make you believe you were unlovable? Did they whisper that you would never be more than your worst mistake or your family's worst mistake?

Somewhere along the way, many of us have tied our worthiness to something other than our creator. And so we've lived with armor to protect us from the world and ourselves.

The bathroom floor strips us of this armor we once thought protected us. And this is a gift, because that armor prevents us from fully living.

This is why we need to go back. Back to those cold tiles that caught our tears, back to those walls where the armor came off and our bare souls were all we had left.

Maybe you sat on those tiles only days ago. Or maybe your unexpected moment was years ago, but you skipped the bathroom floor. Maybe you tried to push through the pain instead of letting it push you deeper.

Whatever the case may be, go back.

Because this journey of undergoing the unexpected requires us to examine ourselves curled up on the shower floor. We need to look at that person with empathy. We need to examine the false constructs she built around her identity. What armor was she using to protect herself? What armor was she wearing that kept her from living wholeheartedly?

It's necessary to go back and sit in that steamy room before we can move forward.

The bathroom floor may have us breaking apart, but it also offers us the opportunity to break apart the lies we believed about ourselves long ago and may carry with us still.

The bathroom floor may have us breaking apart, but it also offers us the opportunity to break apart the lies we believed about ourselves long ago and may carry with us still.

The bathroom floor can help us walk back to who we really were before the world ever told us differently.

The bathroom floor is devastating, yes. But it is also an opportunity. It allows us to examine the shame we carry deep down, the lies we've lived with that tell us we aren't worthy of the connection we all desire. The bathroom floor is an opportunity to then shed the armor we've worn to protect ourselves from these deceits. The armor that has kept us in line so that we behave. Or the armor we've used to try to control every possible outcome. Or the armor that made sure we'd keep achieving and never rest. Or the armor that helped us live small so we could be worthy.

The bathroom floor is where we recognize the armor and begin to take it off piece by piece. It's where we can connect with the living water and allow it to wash us clean once more.

And when we emerge from the floor, when our eyes and our skin have dried, we're given a fresh start to live vulnerably anew. We're given the opportunity to live into the fullness of ourselves.

The bathroom floor can help us live in a whole new way— wide open.

As Brené Brown suggests, although learning to live vulnerably can be difficult, it allows us to experience the fullness of love. To show up as ourselves and find the places where we truly belong. To hope more. To live with more empathy. And to find more meaning.[5] Living vulnerably is key to helping us return to ourselves—the ones God created with intention.

This is the path we take from the bathroom floor. It will be steep, and it will require much, but it will also give us much.

By going back, by owning our whole story, we can eventually move forward as the wholehearted people we want to be. We can eventually move forward with the purpose of living into our God-dreamed entirety.

The baby growing inside me would strip me of my armor. He would out me, he would show me a better way, and he would teach me how to show up just as I am. My body was shaping him, but one day he would shape me.

One day.

I believe your unexpected life holds this potential for you if you are willing to be brave, if you are willing to be vulnerable.

Go back to the bathroom floor. Spend time there. Don't skip over this part. Because when you shed the tears, when you un-leash your innermost thoughts to the One who always hears, when you ask the hard questions, when you sit under the confusion and the weight of your reality in this present moment, you're building up your courage to go deeper still.

By going back, by owning our whole story, we can eventually move forward as the wholehearted people we want to be.

You will be strong enough to go back further in the timeline of your life. You will have the courage to go back and see where you have been and how it has shaped your beliefs, your relationships, and your grief so far. Go back and run your fingers along the armor you wore for so long. And then take that armor and put it where it belongs—in the history book of your life. You don't need to wear it going forward; it no longer fits you. Shed the weight it added to your strong and delicate spine. The armor never protected you anyway; it only held you back from being you.

Let the cold tiles beneath your body be the foundation for a new way of living. You can be brave. You can be vulnerable. You can be you—the you your creator formed long ago. Go back so you can move forward into who He always dreamed you'd be brave enough to be.

Go back to the bathroom floor and break apart so you can break open.

Go back so you can be free.

- *Who was I then?*
  Did I spend time on the bathroom floor? If so, what did I believe about myself? And how did these beliefs shape my grief?

- *Who am I now?*
  Am I still the person on the bathroom floor who believed the lie that I was worthy of connection only if I followed some unspoken rules laid out by society? Or am I living with more vulnerability? In either case, why or why not?

- *Who do I want to become?*
  What armor do I need to remove in order to live wholeheartedly as myself, as the person God intended me to be?

2

Inherent Worth

She was new, and she was free. She did not yet have a name; she had no need for one, because she was known. She lived among the world's richest green plants and vibrant blooms. The animals, she ruled over. The waters glistened from the sun's soft rays, and they were hers to dip her toes into. She could immerse herself there, unclothed, uninhibited, and unashamed. The trees were lush and lively—except for one that promised death.

One day a serpent slid up to her and whispered promises. There was more to this life than she knew, he said. She was missing out, in want, and not free after all. His words made her feel small.

What if there is more? What if I should be more? she thought.

She walked her bare feet over to the tree he planted in her mind and examined its smooth trunk. It did not look like death but life. She ran her fingertips over its ample branches, then reached for its fruit, fruit that looked delicious with new possibilities, and had her fill.

Now I will be more.[1]

I know the feeling well.

43

I have always loved my name. I realize that's not something I'm supposed to say, but it's true. As a child I had a small table and a bench that both read *Jillian* in all caps. My great-uncle Benny was a carpenter and made them just for me. He carved my name into the pine, stained it red, and painted the letters white.

That's where I ate Eggo waffles with extra powdered sugar while my ninety-year-old great-grandmother, Mum-Mum, watched me after preschool. She spent her days ironing and folding laundry for our family of six while my parents worked. She also read me Dr. Seuss's *Green Eggs and Ham* as many times as I requested. Between bites of sugary bread, our reading books, and my watching scenes from *The Muppets*, I ran my tiny index finger inside the bench's deeply grooved letters, knowing it was special and believing my name—and somehow I—was special too.

I would be more.

On Christmas Eve, I waved my shiny patent leather shoes back and forth, back and forth—my feet not even close to touching the church floor—while sitting on a maroon-cushioned pew and wearing a red puffy-sleeved dress complete with a pilgrim-like white collar. It was the early '90s, after all.

In the middle of the service, the main pastor, who had donned a white robe and wore gold-rimmed glasses, stepped down from the pulpit while the choir sang. He kneeled and whispered to me, "Jillian, would you like to sing a solo of 'Away in a Manger'?"

"You only want the one song?" I asked without an ounce of hesitation.

My tiny Mary Janes carried my four-year-old frame to the stage. I waited for my cue and then broke out my impromptu performance with ease.

Titusville, Florida, is a small town. Back then, the space center was one of the only industries in the riverfront city. When teachers went through their first day's *Let's get to know each other* routine, they always asked, "Whose parents work at the Cape?" Only I and maybe one or two other students kept our hands down. Titusville wasn't so small that you knew everyone shopping at the Winn-Dixie, but you had to plan for at least one small-talk encounter every time you left the house. And because it was a small town, if you knew me, you knew I could sing.

Mr. Coppola was new to Titusville, but he'd spotted my talent right away. A few months into my fifth-grade year, Mr. C directed a musical called *How to Eat Like a Child*. Before he assigned official roles for the performance, he made an announcement. "'The Birthday Song' goes to the best singer in the school, and that means it goes to Jillian." A smile spread across my face with abandon.

My mom took me to Limited Too to pick out a brightly colored outfit at Mr. C's instruction. I selected a turquoise top and shorts, complete with rainbow striping. It couldn't have been any louder, and I matched.

The night of the performance, we gathered on the small elementary school stage. The cafeteria lights dimmed, and the stage lights were in full effect. I waited through more than half of the play for it to be my turn.

When I ended the final note—believing the lyrics that said my parents and I were glad I was born were written for me—I was sure the world was glad I'd been born too. Everyone in it smiled at me, just as the audience was smiling at me now.

Like an umbilical cord, the microphone gave me life. My identity was wrapped up in its amplifying wiring both when

I sang as a child and when I eventually became a news anchor as an adult. I felt my best while elevated above others, just out of reach, in the glow of the stage and studio lights.

This made me more. I was sure of it.

My life had always been a bit shiny. I was popular growing up, schoolwork came relatively easy to me, I had a good singing voice, and later, I had a TV job people deemed cool. I thought the move to Alamogordo, New Mexico, which meant the loss of my TV career, and now having a baby with a disability, stripped away my luster.

This is difficult to admit. I know now, but didn't know then, how off base my beliefs about worth were. I know now how wrong I was about disability. I know this now. But back then I thought what made me shiny had disappeared. I thought I'd become dull.

Not only had the small spotlight that followed me during my youth and young adulthood faded, but the bulb had burst, and I was walking barefoot on the shards of glass left behind. The pain reminded me of what I once had and who I once was.

I thought I was no longer envied but pitied.

I thought I was no longer more but less.

I wonder if your unexpected circumstance has left you feeling the same—lost. Has it left you feeling less when the world screams at you to be more?

After years of observing my grief, I believe many of these feelings are spurred by three words: the American Dream.

D. L. Mayfield is the author of *The Myth of the American Dream*, and she sums up the myth this way: "Its most basic iteration goes like this: anyone can make something of themselves if only they try hard enough."[2] My whole life I had tried to earn my way into being more, of being worthy of what others would call a success. I believed my worth was directly tied to my accomplishments, as if I couldn't have the former without the latter. I believed my success, and therefore my worth, was entirely up to me. I defined my worth the American way instead of the godly way.

I know I'm not alone.

A 2019 Populace and Gallup study asked Americans how they believed society perceives success by order of importance. Relationship status took the largest portion of the pie at 45.9 percent, education came in the next largest at 19.8 percent, followed by income level at 8.8 percent whereas personal character was only at 4.9 percent.[3] I bought into and lived out the lie that the American way of success was the only way I could be deemed worthy.

Have you? Have you forgotten where your worth truly comes from?

The unexpected has a way of stripping us bare. Maybe it's left you without the marriage you once cherished. Maybe it's left you with a field of broken dreams. Maybe your identity was tied to something, someone, now lost. Without that person or thing, without the shine you once had, you stand naked with what's left—you.

Maybe you're standing where I once stood. Your feet still take you to your bathroom mirror every morning, but you don't recognize the person staring back at you. Your eyes are still the same color, your mouth still curves in its peculiar way, but behind those familiar features are questions. Who lives here in this unknown place? Is she still important? Does her life still matter?

If I could go back—back to my old bathroom in my Alamogordo home, back to staring at the red eyes looking back at me perched above a heavy belly and even heavier heart—I would tell myself this: *Don't sit still. Go back. Go back to the very beginning, and you'll see that your worth was settled long ago.*

Like those in the Gallup study, back then I also thought marital status, education, and income level were crucial to a successful and therefore worthy life.

Crucial to being more.

So how could my son, a person with an intellectual disability, ever have a life that was successful and therefore worthy?

A few months before our son was conceived, Andy and I flew to Florida for what will likely be the most spectacular wedding we'll ever attend. If there were a show called *My Celebrity-Style Wedding*, these nuptials would take top nods. The ceremony and reception were held at the bride's family's multi-million-dollar beachfront estate, with several bands, dozens of food stations, and even synchronized swimmers in the backyard pool. From the flowers to the lights and the warm beignets they served at departure, every detail was meant to seep into the guests' memories.

But something the rabbi said as he united my friend with his bride left the biggest mark. Under a clear chuppah covered in flowing white linens overlooking the Atlantic, he said, "Marriage is not the most important thing; it is the *only* important thing."

I squeezed Andy's hand, believing the statement was both beautiful and true.

Not long after our son's final diagnosis, Andy and I lay in bed, and he took my hand and looked at me with tears in his eyes. He was barely able to speak.

"What's wrong?" I asked, panicked.

Andy's tears started to fall with such force that his throat began to close. Then he managed to choke out a sentence I will never forget. "I hope he meets a girl with Down syndrome. I want him to love someone the way I love you." My heart both swelled with gratitude for my husband and burst under the weight of his grief.

His grief was my own.

Neither of us could imagine our son living a fulfilling life without a marriage like the one we shared. And if I'm being honest, nor without the degrees we'd earned and the material wealth we were building. Our beliefs matched so many of those in that Gallup poll, and so I thought success was out of reach for my unborn child and therefore for me too. It left me feeling worthless.

Much of what lessened my grief in the last weeks of pregnancy and the first weeks of my son's life were stories that made me believe he could achieve the things I valued despite his disability. I assumed disability was something to overcome instead of an intrinsic part of who my son was. Reading about the hundreds of college programs for young adults with intellectual disabilities and couples with Down syndrome marrying had me high on the possibility that his life could look just like my own.

Opportunity and relationships are, of course, wonderful. And I should add, possible for people with disabilities. Yet these stories gave me hope because they matched the checklist of the American Dream, where marriage and intelligence are foundational to a successful and therefore worthy life.

But success and worth are two entirely different things. And in the upside-down world of Jesus, living out a successful life is very different if not the opposite of the American Dream. It's helping those who can't help you and loving those who hate you. It's a life of giving yourself away instead of building yourself up. A successful life is not about climbing up the ladder but down. Character does not make up a mere 4.9 percent of the life God desires for us to co-create with Him. Our character changes when we are so in touch with the Divine, when His presence flows through us, when He shapes our internal and then our external lives.

Maybe you're not measuring up to what the world values, but what God values is attainable. Because He breaks through in us. He loves us as we are, and He loves us enough to call us into the work of transformation. This is the work of love, and it invites us inward and outward. This is the work, I believe, Jesus deems successful. It's work I believe becomes more apparent after being hit by the unexpected.

The world's elite—those strong in legalism and weak in love, who couldn't see they were sick and in need of help—were the people Jesus rejected. They were the ones He said missed the point because they elevated themselves, cared more about their worldly status, and lived by the rules of men—strong in pretenses and weak in mercy.

I had missed the point.

The church often misses the point too.

A recent study found that two-thirds of Protestants say God wants them to prosper, and one in four say they have to do something for God in order to receive material blessings in return.[4] This is called "the prosperity gospel." It's easy to spot when watching megachurch preachers on TV selling it—*God will bless you if you give back to Him!* It's harder to spot when that Americanized message has infiltrated our hearts. When we think we have to perform to receive God's approval, His love. But when we think we have to live out the hallmarks of the American Dream to be called worthy, we've missed the heart of God while breaking our own in the process.

Again, it was hard for me to picture my son having a life as fulfilling as ours without a love that looked like the one his dad and I shared. But now, years later, I believe the rabbi who presided over my friend's stunning wedding got it wrong. Marriage isn't the only thing. Love is. Maybe our son won't love someone the way his dad and I love each other, but he will love, and he will be loved. He will love his sister, his younger brother, his grandparents, his cousins—and maybe even a wife. He is and will continue to be so very loved by God. Married or unmarried, our son's life will be full of love.

Your worth isn't attached to your resume.

I didn't know it when I was grieving over his diagnosis, but I soon discovered his worth will never be attached to his resume. It took me even longer to realize my worth isn't attached to my resume.

Your worth isn't attached to your resume, either.

Understanding this truth was hard-earned for me. It took digging and digging some more to not just find it but to sit with it. Then one day, as I'll show you in the pages ahead, this truth began wrapping me in its peace with the small curl of a smile.

This is why I'm asking you to undergo the unexpected instead of overcome it. I want you to dig and then sit with these truths for a while, because I believe you will not only read about them now but will one day be open enough for them to be imprinted on your soul.

Here are the lie and the truth I want you to sit with: The world has us believe our worth comes from our accomplishments, our intellect, our attachments. Our worth, however, is born out of love, God's love for us. Nothing can add to our worth, and nothing can take it away.

Because it was promised from the very beginning.

--------- **The Gift** ---------

We often mesh the two creation stories in Genesis 1 and 2 into one. Many of us grew up hearing the story of the weak woman and the deceptive serpent and how the perfect world God created was ruined by both. Then there's the one that focuses on the order God made things, the number of days it took Him, His rest, and yes, also the woman who brought the world down with her. We've heard the stories so many times that our brains can hardly process the sacred words. *We know, we know*, we think when our devotionals lead us back to the start.

Whether we take the creation stories literally or allegorically (and I encourage you to make conclusions about this through your own study) matters less than what we can learn from the text, especially the parts we often overlook. We get caught up in the details and miss the promises. The promises in Genesis 1 and 2 are these: God created, and He calls all His creations very good. Adam and Eve were not worthy because they accomplished many things; they were worthy because they belonged to God. They were His.

We are good not because of what we do or don't do but because of who we are—His.

After God tells Adam and Eve the natural consequences of their sin, He sends the couple away. But before they're evicted from the garden, God clothes them. In doing so, He promises to love them, to care for them. Although they will no longer see Him, He will see them. He will not let them go as they walk away.

The unexpected forces us to walk out of our gardens—the way we believe life could have been, the way we believe life should have been. But as we take steps along our unexpected path, we can begin a journey back toward God and back toward ourselves. Our true selves that God has already deemed so very worthy.

When life falls apart, the things we tie our worth to often shatter along with it. For me, it was my accomplishments, my worldly status. Maybe it is for you too. Or maybe a relationship, a job, or an ability was taken away. As we exit our gardens—whether by our own doing or because something simply happened—there will be sadness. There will be grief.

But if you choose to keep your eyes open, if you choose to undergo this unexpected experience instead of overcoming it, there can also be an awakening.

The creation stories show us we were never going to live perfect lives. There was always going to be heartache and pain here on earth, mistakes both big and small. But thank God, He loves us anyway.

We can do nothing to add to our inherent worth.

We can do nothing to lessen our inherent worth.

And nothing done to us can mean God has deemed us unworthy.

We will live out the consequences of our sin—or simply the consequences of being human—but He clothes us and watches over us as we walk out of our former lives and into our unexpected new ones. And we walk there covered by His love.

My son would change how I view worth. Little by little, he would change my long-held notions about self-sufficiency, intelligence, and status. Little by little, he would open up my soul. He would help me find my way back to myself, the girl on that tiny bench who God had already deemed worthy, not because of what she could do but because she belonged to Him.

Even if . . .

Nothing on the end of that phrase could make my son less worthy to me. I love him for all he is, and I will love him for all he will become.

Even if . . .

How much more must your creator feel that way about you?

You are worthy because you are here, and you are worthy because you are His. Nothing can take that away. Not the job loss, not the betrayal, not the illness—or if you're like I was, not that unexpected thing your heart just can't quite understand yet but one day will. Nothing.

> You are worthy because you are here, and you are worthy because you are His. Nothing can take that away.

That 2019 Gallup survey also found that while most Americans believe society defines success to be status-oriented, less than 10 percent of participants applied this standard to their own definition of success.[5] Instead, they had a highly unique, personal view of success. It seems we're desperate to break free from the world's standards.

I believe the unexpected can help us untangle ourselves from the world's definition of worth and instead help us find it in our beginnings. The story of us begins with a God who has called us very good from the day He first breathed us into life.

No unexpected circumstance can take this truth away from you. Instead, if you let it, it has the power to reveal this truth to you. I didn't need the stage or studio lights to be more. And as days turned into months, I would learn that my son, not yet born, would never need to accomplish the things of this world to be more.

And neither do we.

THE *Gift* OF *You*

* *Who was I then?*
  How did I view my worth in the heat of my unexpected moment? How did my views affect my grief?

* *Who am I now?*
  Do Western ideas affect how I see myself, my unexpected moment, my worth? If so, how so?

* *Who do I want to become?*
  What ideas do I need to shed to believe I am worthy just because I'm God's creation? How would living like I'm worthy change my life?

3

Deconstruction

I was afraid of the dark as a child. There's nothing unique about that. I don't remember fearing monsters under my bed, though. It was just a general angst. I was afraid an unnamed something or someone might get me in the absence of day. The fear continued well past the appropriate time and into high school. If I was home alone at night, I turned on every light in the house, darting for the nearest switch as fast as my legs allowed. I feared the dark because of the unknowns that could be waiting in its shadows.

But in those initial days of grief, it was daylight that scared me. The mornings were always the worst. At night, I was thankful for pregnancy-induced fatigue and fell asleep without struggle. But then the Southwestern sun would rise over the mountains and shine too brightly on our reality all over again. The phone call, the doctor's speech, the amniocentesis results—none of it had been a dream.

He really has Down syndrome.

The doctor's words looped in my head over and over again like a slideshow of photographs playing at a wake. I kept seeing flashes of what my son's life could never be. The doctor's speech was like a bad drug dripping in my veins, and I didn't realize the medicine was actually poison because I'd never seen a different outcome. Growing up, I hadn't known anyone with Down syndrome or any significant disability.

He won't be able to learn. He won't have friends. He won't be able to contribute to society.

He won't, he won't, he won't.

I feared my son would be an eternal child, never experiencing the fullness life offers. I pictured him living a life of exclusion, meeting rejection at every step. I imagined him living a less-than existence, forced to walk in the shadow of what could have been. Our son would live his days on the margins of society, and I had only ever occupied its center. I wanted nothing less for my child, but I couldn't do anything about his standing in the world.

My son's life was already written, already decided. Sadness was all I could see printed on his book's pages. I kept letting that doctor's bias course through my bloodstream, killing every ounce of hope and weakening my heart little by little. I believed his words because I'd only seen children with intellectual disabilities live a separate life, tucked away in a different classroom. They lived on the side of "them," the sad side. I didn't know there was another way, a better way, so the poison kept flowing.

Drip, drip, drip.

Injustice ruled my thoughts.

Why me?

Why us? We live decently enough. We're kind enough. We give enough.

How did we end up here in this wasteland with a baby whose life is over before it begins?

How could God pull the rug out from under us when we trusted Him? Aren't His plans supposed to be good? Our lives were just getting started, and now they're over too.

Injustice would then slide into guilt.

I did this to him.

I wasn't kind enough growing up. I made fun of Roger in the sixth grade. I went off on a friend in front of the whole middle school. I could have used my social power in high school to reach out to kids who were struggling. God is punishing me. I deserve this.

I don't have enough humility. God is humbling me.

My mind charged up through anger and slid down into shame over and over like a roller coaster I couldn't get off of. I'd air out my grievances toward God and then rage against myself. God felt distant, and I was in a space I no longer recognized.

The place was dark even when daylight shined. There was no switch to make me feel secure. What I once feared was waiting for me in the shadows was now out, exposed, attacking me around every corner.

"*Coming,*" Mrs. Porter[1] said during a spelling test.

She paused for a long time as I, and the rest of her second-grade class, began writing out the word with our sharpened number 2 pencils.

"*Coming.* . . . Some of you think Santa is *coming* on Christmas Eve, but Jesus is *coming.*"

I stopped believing Santa was behind all the gifts on Christmas morning when I was seven. To be fair, it wasn't all because of Mrs. Porter's spelling example. I went to a strict Christian elementary school where Santa talk was not allowed. Santa was the lie that stole Christmas; believing in him was taking away from Jesus. Santa was evil, and so were many other things. In the midst of spelling out all the evils in the world, g-r-a-c-e was absent from the classroom.

I'm sure it was there somewhere. But it's not what stuck out in my young mind.

~~~~~~

I was surrounded by green. My Florida home was green, too, but not like this. The Appalachians stretched and peaked as far as the eye could see, enveloping me in life. But a death awaited.

My best friend, Cassie,[2] invited me to a church camp in North Carolina the summer between fifth and sixth grades. The place was a kid wonderland. It lured me—us—in with its giant fort, massive water slide, and rock wall. As though it were a piece of bait dangling within my grasp, I thought I was about to receive a good gift. But it was a trick. The camp leaders had me on the line and reeled me into a theology that would leave me flailing for years to come.

The day before I boarded a bus to go, my mom had to take me shopping for knee-length shorts. These were the days before Bermudas and capris were in style. The only option I had was to go to the boys' department. I reluctantly bought a pair of mesh basketball shorts and two pairs of plaid shorts striped with earth tones. But on the first morning of camp, I was walking from my cabin to a lecture hall when a male employee patrolling the grounds sent me back to change. My baggy, unfitting, and already unsightly shorts weren't quite long enough.

I walked into the lecture hall late and was confused by the slide on the projection screen. On it was a list of G-rated slang terms. The graphic explained how even these seemingly innocent words are sinful because, it said, they're a derivative of the word *God*. Saying *goodness*, *golly*, or *gosh* was taking the Lord's name in vain.

Later, we hiked to a nearby waterfall. The trail was steep, and at one point we had to hold on to a skinny tree to shimmy our eleven-year-old bodies down a drop-off to make it to our destination. Being used to Florida's flat land, I was intimidated and said "Oh my gosh" as I tried to wrestle myself to the lower level of the trail.

A camp instructor snapped, "Watch your language!"

I was normally the teacher's pet; I rarely got into trouble. Here, I couldn't stay out of trouble.

I'm sure the waterfall was beautiful, but the sight of it ran right through me. My camp mates splashed around in the natural pool, but I couldn't shake off the shame of my newly learned sin. I was dry.

So I raised my hand at the nightly gathering and got "saved." I had already been "saved," but I wasn't sure if it counted now.

The counselor said, "Today, July 30, 1998,[3] you can tell the devil you won't be going with him because you will always have this day."

Apparently, it took only one prayer to keep Satan away; the side of guilt and unattainable rule-following were for added measure. The sun was setting over the mountains, filling the sky with brilliant pinks and oranges. I sat there staring at the serene scene confused because the release I was hoping for hadn't come. I was filled with messages, and the messages told me I was dirty and would never be good enough for God or good enough for this place.

Cassie hugged me. The adults hugged me. I was somehow part of God's family now, but I'd never felt so distant from myself.

I walked back to my cabin as night fell, my knees wobbly and my mind as dark as the sky. The guilt inside me was churning, thickening, becoming something new—anger.

The final night of camp, the leaders instructed us to grab a stick and toss it into a campfire. We were to do this only if we were ready to be done with our sinful ways and live anew in God.

I didn't get up.

I sat alone in my chair, heavy. I would not be moved. I had been pushed too far. I noticed one other camper maybe six rows up who also sat. I only saw the back of his brown, coifed hair, but I felt something I hadn't since crossing the Carolina border—solidarity. I wasn't the only one questioning. I wasn't the only one who felt something about this place was off. I wished he could see me too. I wanted him to know he wasn't alone.

Jesus paid it all on the cross, but that didn't appear to be enough. The camp's focus was on sin and not the love that covered it. The faith that was handed to me focused on retribution and missed the redemption. This religion wanted right behavior. Like the religious elite Jesus called out while on earth, they focused on the rules and missed the heart of the Ruler. He came to show us that God is love, and loving Him means a transformation of the heart, not the destruction of its vessels.

But there was no heart in the mountains, just unforgiving terrain leading to an unopened tomb.

From what I remember about my early exposure to Christianity, it lacked the first part of the word—*Christ*. Instead, it was built on the pillars of hate and evil. To hate what was evil. God was to be feared. He was the ultimate punisher and rewarder.

Religion was a transaction.

Coming to faith as an adult didn't happen for me in an instant. There was no special prayer that tethered my heart to the One who made me. It took a series of encounters.

I had always kept a toe in the water. I believed there was a God; I just wasn't sure if the Christians had it right. By the time Andy and I were seriously dating, I had maybe a whole foot in. I admired his church upbringing, and he admired my questions, some he had never asked. We danced in the water.

We pushed and pulled each other, him spinning me out to the deep, me turning back to the shallows when my eyes caught a glimpse of the childhood church scars I still wore.

⁓⁓⁓

I forced his hand into granting the interview.

I left a message with Dan Brown's secretary, letting her know we attended Trinity on the Hill United Methodist Church and I wanted him to give me an interview for a news piece I was putting together for the sweeps rating period. The story was about a group that believed the world was ending on May 21, 2011. They'd even paid for billboard messages alerting people to the rapture. It was an easy story, marketable, and it gave me an excuse to interview the pastor Andy and I had been listening to every Sunday morning for the past few months.

"I believe people live in hell every day," Dan said to me.

Dan is a large man, well over six feet tall and barrel-chested, with an enviable head of thick white hair. His voice is like velvet, and his words connect almost as if he's singing as he speaks. He was warm, and his words were too.

I sensed he knew I was interviewing him more for myself than for my TV story.

"How would you describe a separation from God?" he asked me. He explained his beliefs about biblical writers using intense symbolic language to describe hopelessness and despair.

My mind flashed back to *Heaven's Gates and Hell's Flames*, a play Cassie's church had put on. It featured scenes of dying sinners with both those who had repented and those who hadn't. The "saved" ones were welcomed through the pearly gates with open arms. But the unsaved people's names couldn't be found in the Book of Life. The lights went out, a strobe light started flashing, the music grew haunting, and the devil himself came out to escort these souls into an eternity of torture.

The play, of course, ended with an altar call—the call to repent and forever be saved from the fiery pit of hell. There was no loving people to Jesus. It wasn't even *scaring* them into His arms. I'm not sure how much Jesus was a factor in it at all. The play and the churches I grew up around frightened people into a way of life, giving them a list of rules they had to follow in order to avoid damnation. They focused on "saving" as many people as possible but never made those people feel safe.

My photographer, Dominic, had Dan perfectly framed. The afternoon light poured through the stained-glass windows in the upper corner of his shot, and heaven was breaking through.

Again, I encourage you to study for yourself, seeking answers to any questions you have about what the Bible says and any theological issue. But the hell I was exposed to as a child didn't fit with the God I had learned about in my later years; I could never reconcile the two. And that day, Dan showed me there is more to Jesus than the threat or promise of an afterlife. He painted a new picture for me, where mercy flows, forgiveness is abundant, radical love reigns, and God can extend grace to anyone.

It was time to leave the church of my past and the resentment behind. I moved one foot in front of the other, stepping deeper into the water.

Soon after, I read a blurb in the church bulletin advertising a nine-month-long intensive study that covered more than 80 percent of the Bible. I pointed to it and whispered to Andy, "We have to go." I had to investigate Christianity like the journalist I was if it were ever to become part of my life outside of Sunday mornings, and I needed Andy to sit beside me during the process.

Dan led the group and took us through the laws and prophecies of the Messiah, then finally through every recorded word

Jesus spoke. They were words filled with love, not wrath like I'd believed all those years ago. Dan put historical and literary context behind the library that is the Bible. Christianity wasn't built on hate and fear; it was built on a God who is love, and that love spurs Him to do the work of restoration.

The religious elite of the past missed the point. The people in my past missed the point.

I had missed Him too.

The Gift

Even though I had lost my faith and found a new one, my old faith came creeping back when the unexpected hit.

This is where I will once again tell you that my views on disability and Down syndrome were rooted in my ignorance, fear, and ableism. I thought Down syndrome was an illness. I thought my son needed healing. And it would take me many months to see Down syndrome not as something that took away from my unborn child but was in every part of making him into who he was and who he would one day be.

When you're hit by the unexpected, the force can shake your foundation. For me, the new foundation I stood on still needed to be sealed. And so it broke open, and the weeds down below peaked through the cracks.

I still couldn't help but wonder if God was punishing me for my past and present, my self-centeredness, my quest for position and need for attention. I had recently studied the Creator as all-loving, but I didn't *know* Him that way. My heart was operating off the quid pro quo God economy I grew up with— God punishes the bad and blesses the good.

I wonder if your faith is operating off that same perception of God. I wonder if someone told you that sinners suffer and saints do not. I'm not sure how we ever came to this conclusion when most of Jesus's disciples were martyred. I'm not sure how we think suffering is God's punishment for sin when God Himself was tortured on a cross.

You see, I believe Jesus came here to show us not only who God is but how we got God wrong. He came to show us the full picture of God. He came not to inflict pain but to be with us in it. He wept.[4] Jesus came not to punish but to shock us into the depth of His love with arms stretched wide.

The unexpected would eventually unravel the final thread that tied me to the church of my past.

Perhaps you didn't grow up with the fire-and-brimstone version of God like I did. But with the infiltration of the American Dream in churches and the rise of the prosperity gospel we discussed in the last chapter, maybe the quid pro quo God is the God you know.

Maybe you think your life, your faith, is a series of transactions. Maybe you're trying to rack up good deeds so you will be blessed and avoid bad deeds so you won't be cursed. Maybe you think you have to earn God's love and deserve whatever unexpected thing that has happened to you. Or perhaps you think you've lived well enough and don't understand why you, who has been faithful, are in a place you don't recognize. In a place you don't want to be.

> I believe Jesus came here to show us not only who God is but how we got God wrong. He came to show us the full picture of God. He came not to inflict pain but to be with us in it.

I believe the unexpected can help us deconstruct any faulty faith we have and help us rebuild a faith where Jesus is the foundation.

The type of Christianity I was exposed to growing up stems from the fundamentalist movement. Fundamentalism began in the late nineteenth century, and its leaders branded this new, individualistic, "plain and literal" reading of the Bible as an "old-time religion" movement.[5] Fundamentalism de-emphasized scholarship and emphasized sin, salvation, and inerrancy.

One of the problems I see with the fundamentalist's legalistic view of Scripture is that it doesn't give us tools we need to examine the harsh parts of the Bible, the wrath we see in the Old Testament. It also doesn't account for the lens through which the reader is interpreting the Bible.

C. S. Lewis wrote this in regard to the Bible and interpreting it:

> The total result is not "the Word of God" in the sense that every passage, in itself, gives impeccable science or history. It carries the Word of God and we (under grace, with attention to tradition and to interpreters wiser than ourselves and with the use of such intelligence and learning as we may have) receive that word from it not by using it as an encyclopedia or an encyclical but by steeping ourselves in its tone and temper and so learning its overall message.[6]

Instead of God being the God of grace and love and the deliverer of the oppressed, the overall message I received from my fundamentalist-church schooling was that God was vengeful and exclusionary, and damnation was just one wrong step away.

My goal here is not to convert you to my own theological views but to help you examine the faith message you've received and the lens through which you're currently viewing the Bible and God. Because whether or not we know it, we read the

Bible through a personalized lens formed by the people who handed their faith down to us—parents, teachers, or perhaps leaders from a church we once attended. As Miguel De La Torre writes, this lens also comprises our social status, culture, and community.[7]

In his book *Reading the Bible from the Margins*, De La Torre explains this further: "To claim objectivity in biblical interpretations is to mask the subjectivity of the person, groups, or culture doing the interpreting. The interpretation of Scripture can never occur apart from the identity of the one doing the interpreting."[8]

The unexpected can help us—the ones interpreting the Bible—understand ourselves better. When we see ourselves more clearly, we're better equipped to examine the lens through which we view God. When we have a firmer grasp on who we are, when we understand what has shaped us and our views about God, we can break down the false constructs we've built around ourselves and around the One who cannot be contained.

None of us will deconstruct the faith we have, rebuild, and end up with identical structures, because the Bible is not an answer key. God is purposefully mysterious. But we can look at our unexpected situations that have left us questioning the Divine's role in them—that have left us questioning God Himself and cracked the foundation we stand on—and use them to pursue the mystery.

It's easy to go through the motions of faith. We take what's been handed to us without really inspecting its parts. Or perhaps we walk away from our faith completely. But our unexpected moments can help us not only walk toward the faith we have but sink into it, to go deeper than we ever have.

The deeper I examined how I was reacting to my unexpected moment, the more I came to realize that the faith handed to me was built on hell instead of on Jesus. When I started to investigate Christianity, I learned that *hell* is a word Christians created. In his book *The Bible Tells Me So*, professor and author Peter Enns explains that the Hebrew word we often see translated into "hell" is *ge' Hinnom*. Ge' Hinnom, the "Valley of Hinnom," was a valley outside of Jerusalem where that city's residents sacrificed their children to foreign gods.[9] They used their free will to turn their backs on Him. They lived apart from Him.

> **The deeper I examined how I was reacting to my unexpected moment, the more I came to realize that the faith handed to me was built on hell instead of on Jesus.**

It was hell on earth. A hell of people's own making. A hell they chose. Of course, scholars disagree on whether hell is a literal place. My point here is to be cautious when church leaders speak and act out of their certainty of hell instead of the assurance of God's love.

The church leaders of my past expelled so much breath talking of hell, and in doing so, they made their own kind of hell for those who listened—and perhaps for themselves as well. This message created a separation from the God of grace. Their God did not delight in His creations; He tallied all the ways they messed up.

If the faith you know pushes the narrative of retribution instead of the message of God's grace, may I gently suggest that you go back? Go back and start with the words of Jesus. If Jesus was God in flesh, God revealed to us, it changes the Israelites' interpretation of the sometimes-vengeful version of God.

Peter Enns put it this way:

Israel's story, taken on its own terms, is not adequate to bear the weight of God's surprise move of a crucified and resurrected messiah. It must be reshaped around Jesus. If we miss that lesson—if we look to the Bible as a collection of unchanging information about God and miss how the reality of Jesus necessarily transforms Israel's story—we will miss what the earliest Christian writers have to say. We will miss Jesus.[10]

And Jesus did not come to destroy. He came to heal.

In *The Will of God*, Dr. Leslie Weatherhead describes an encounter with a grieving friend whose child has died of cholera. The friend decides the tragic death must have been the will of God. Leslie asks his friend what he would think if someone broke into his house that night and put a cholera-soaked cloth over his other child's face. The man is stunned by his question but concludes he would kill the intruder and throw him off his veranda.

Dr. Weatherhead responds, "Surely we cannot identify as the will of God something for which a man would be locked up in jail."[11]

The story above doesn't pertain to my unexpected moment, the one I have chosen to write this book around, because now I've come to believe a person being born with Down syndrome is not a bad thing. But the story has fit others' unexpected moments. Perhaps it fits yours. If our bathroom-floor moments have us believing God must be punishing us—that He created this destruction, this illness, this accident, this betrayal for some reason we cannot see—maybe it's time to stop blaming Him and start believing Him instead.

Are we going to believe God when He says our sins have been paid for and that this idea of retribution goes against what He has already done for us?[12] Are we going to believe Him when

He says He has overcome the world? Are we going to believe Him when He says He came not to steal but to give us life?

Are we going to believe Him?

When we believe Jesus embodies the essence of the Divine, we can let go of the shame and blame surrounding our unexpected circumstances and find rest in His outstretched arms, recognizing the promise they bring—redemption.

Pain is a result of being human. But our unexpected hurts are not the end.

Thank God for that.

Let us sink deeply into the foundation we're standing on. Let's find the parts of our faith that need to stay, the parts that need to go, and ask God to help us see what new materials need to be added.

It may feel like you're breaking, but Jesus is a carpenter. He can take the faith of our past and our present questions and cover them. He can help us transform the foundation we have into something that withstands.

Because *He* withstands.

THE *Gift* OF *You*

- *Who was I then?*
  At the darkest point in my grief. Meaning, how did I view God and His role in my trial and the trials of others?

- *Who am I now?*
  What is shaping the lens through which I read the Bible and in turn view the Divine? (Consider the faith that was handed to you, your culture, your worldly status.)

- *Who do I want to become?*
  What do I need to unlearn and learn about my creator to make Jesus the center of my faith? What would it take to stop blaming God and start believing that He came to give us life, not take it away?

4

Uniquely Loved

Decaf Coffee Night transpired after my cousin Caroline's failed bachelorette party. Well, the party didn't exactly fail; I just failed to make it there.

We were living in Las Vegas at the time, and Caroline was driving up from Phoenix with a car full of friends to celebrate her upcoming nuptials. I texted her several times trying to determine the plan, but the girls were young and ready to go wherever the valley winds took them.

Caroline texted just after eight o'clock, once they'd decided on a place for dinner. I'd been a sophomore in college the last time a night started that late for me, and I had a choice—either make the thirty-minute drive to the strip to hang out with a bunch of tipsy bachelorettes and later the thirty-minute drive home, or pass. I was a tired parent and annoyed by how drastic the four-year age gap between my cousin and me had become.

I decided to stay home. But it was still Friday night, and I still wanted to have some fun before turning in at a reasonable hour.

We'll make cocktails, and we'll listen to some music, I thought. *It will still feel like it's the weekend.*

That's when Andy had the nerve to brew himself a cup of decaf coffee.

"Decaf coffee? It's Friday night! Why are you making coffee? Are we this old? Should we go to bed right now? How did we get here?" I whined.

"Jill, I'm a grown man. If I want decaf coffee, I'll have decaf coffee."

He wasn't entertaining my emotional outburst. But I kept going, trying to peel back the layers of the certain quarter-life crisis upon us.

I knew I was being ridiculous. I could hear the stream of nonsensical words flowing from my mouth. But like a kid who had one too many sweets before boarding a fair ride, I couldn't keep from spewing.

When Andy tells the story now, he gives me a Hulk voice, and it's not far off. I thought he would be happy I was staying home, but instead, he thought I was robbing his worn-out, residency-riddled mind of his early bedtime plans. Andy was rarely mad at me, but I had gone too far.

There was only one way for me to recover—sex. Great sex. And that's what we did. I didn't make him wear protection because one wild session would be fine, right? The rebellion of it even dialed down my self-prescribed uncool factor after the bachelorette debacle.

Yet as I stepped out of bed and into the shower, worry washed over me. *What if Decaf Coffee Night has a lasting effect?* I scrubbed my scalp with shampoo, and the fear went down the drain. Then as I started lathering with conditioner, the fear was replaced by fantasy. It had taken us so long to get pregnant with Violet that to not have to try to conceive might be nice.

While my mind spun from angst to enthusiasm beneath the warm water, a dance was going on inside me. The music began before Andy and I ever met on the dance floor.

Before our cells found each other that night, they were already twirling. While most of them follow the moves of one of those predetermined line dances, one of our cells danced to its own beat, breaking from the group rhythm. The cell, from either my body or Andy's, grooved to a different tune, ignoring the step where it was to split off in perfect pairs, the way most do. When our bodies became entangled on the dance floor, Andy's cell found my unruly one or mine his. Then when we left the dance floor and our bodies separated, the song continued inside me: An embryo with more genetic material than most—an extra copy of the 21st chromosome—kept dancing.

Down syndrome didn't happen to my son. It's always been a part of him.

Days after the amniocentesis results, Andy found me on the floor of Violet's room. I loved her nursery. I'd spent hours crafting purple decorations with her monogram in our North Augusta home, and they were among the very first things we put up in our Las Vegas home. But we had been in our Alamogordo house for weeks, and her room was still barren. It held her crib and clothes, but it was a shell of what it used to be.

Andy sat beside me on the old tan carpet. He was wearing his military uniform, and I had on yoga pants and a blue top that was finally showcasing a taut belly full of life—a new life I didn't feel ready for. I was holding Violet's old sonogram photo and this baby's new one, looking for differences other than the obvious anatomical one, trying to convince myself they weren't there.

They were.

I was exhausted from a day of intense emotions about a future that seemed less certain than before. Really, the future was always uncertain, and a genetic condition didn't make it more so. It just brought the reality to light. The reality that we can control only so much. The reality that we all have a shared delicate condition known as being human.

Andy was tired too. My extroverted, optimistic husband was normally the rally guy at the office. You know, the one who always makes a point of delivering small talk and lightens the mundanity of the nine-to-five routine with a solid dad joke. Now he got his work done and then hid in his car alone, his only lunch companion a daily box of Popeye's chicken.

We were both growing mentally and physically heavier with the passing days.

On this day, he told me about two friends reaching out to him. It was the first time he'd heard anything about their siblings with disabilities. And that really bothered him.

Andy was one of those dreamy guys in high school. He was homecoming king, captain of the football team, and voted "Best All Around." He was also a protector and a defender. He didn't tolerate bullying, and he had the social power to do something about it. His mom once told me a story about some guys on his football team making fun of a kid who was small, a bit different, and had an odd voice. Some of the guys called him Aflac after the duck on the insurance commercials. With one encounter, Andy put an end to it.

As we talked about his friends' previously unknown disabled siblings, he told me he refused to let our son be invisible. "I want everyone to know he's *my* son."

Right then, I knew our baby's name: Anderson—son of Andrew.

Today, I see there is no Anderson without Down syndrome, and there never was. In every cell that makes my son who he is, the extra chromosome is there. I didn't want it to define him, but it did. It does. Now I see this not as a broken reality but a beautifully unique one.

As I mentioned before, when I became pregnant on Decaf Coffee Night at twenty-six, my chance of having a baby with an extra copy of chromosome 21 was one in thousand, 0.1 percent. Anderson's genetic makeup is one in thousand to the world, yet we have a God so vast that He cares for each of us as one in hundreds of billions.

Anderson is one in hundreds of billions to His creator. But while he was still growing inside me, I couldn't see him that way, because I couldn't see myself for who I really was— one in hundreds of billions who have made up the story of humanity. Each of us uniquely made and deeply cared for. Each of us with an important part to write in the story still being written.

Two months before we moved to Alamogordo, I lay on the couch on my mother-in-law's screened-in porch and admitted something so ugly and so true. "I think what hurts the worst about getting the assignment in New Mexico is realizing no one will want my life anymore."

With orders to the middle of nowhere, who was I now? The performing, the writing, the questioning had all led me to the news studio, and now I saw only color bars in my future—the ones that show up on TV when something goes wrong. There wasn't a Target in Alamogordo, let alone a TV station. I didn't know who I was apart from the performer.

I had several crying sessions over my future with Andy. No matter how hard I tried to compute, life didn't seem to add up anymore. I feared that with no eyes on me, I would fade into the background of the world. My hands were rid of a mic, empty

76

of a yellow journalist's pad, and filled with a growing baby and another one on the way.

What goals would I strive for now? I thought people loved me for what I could do, therefore I loved myself for the same reasons. My strengths were tangible for the public to see. I did things worthy of applause every now and again. Now the only applause I got was from a game of patty-cake with my one-year-old. I organized things that didn't need organizing, just hoping Andy would notice. Motherhood is a job with little recognition, and I missed being seen.

That small girl who was so sure there was something special about her name and about her didn't know she would grow up to be ordinary. Without applause, without the studio lights, without the professional and personal highlight reel, I wasn't special anymore.

After I made that confession to Andy's mom, my throat tightened, my back tensed, and my hands grasped my barely-there bump. As the nighttime summer breeze blew through the porch screens and the trees rustled in the background, Debbie didn't know what to say. I didn't blame her. I could hardly believe what I'd just admitted out loud. I was rarely vulnerable.

If I was worried no one would want my life before having a baby with Down syndrome—just because I would be living in a remote area—now I had no doubt. But soon, the baby growing inside me became a mirror. In the days after we named him, Anderson began helping me understand the real me, a woman who had spent years hiding behind the many masks she wore. The me who didn't have to earn her worth but rested in knowing it was already settled.

The rare openness I showed on the porch that night would become my new way of living. In time, I would begin living as myself, my true self. The one the unexpected helped me find.

The Gift

Growing up in a church environment where I was taught my body was bad, my ideas were evil, and my instincts were corrupt, I couldn't see myself as good. The idea of God delighting in me as His unique creation was unbelievable. The notion of His wanting a relationship with me was foreign. I never saw myself as someone He wanted, just someone He wanted to obey Him.

> **I was unable to see myself as God saw me—uniquely loved. Uniquely wanted. Uniquely made for purposes I could not begin to imagine.**

This seed was already planted as I walked away from God. It brought forth a shriveled plant, rooted in lies. I couldn't face the sun, for then I would be seen, for then I would be exposed. I thought the result would be unacceptable.

The lies told me I could not trust myself, so I edited. I edited with makeup and clothes so outsiders always saw me as put together. I edited with behavior, afraid to be real or even silly with anyone outside my innermost circle. I edited with my choices, always keeping one foot on the ground.

I was unable to see myself as God saw me—uniquely loved. Uniquely wanted. Uniquely made for purposes I could not begin to imagine.

Anderson, the unexpected, taught me that our identities are not a mistake but set apart from the very beginning.

When I was still pregnant with Anderson, a mysterious package arrived at my door. I ripped open the sticky gray seal and found a tiny white onesie inside. On the front was a baby-blue circle with Anderson's name inside it. Under his name were the words "Fearfully and Wonderfully Made." I bristled at the Psalm 139 reference. I couldn't believe my mom sent it to me. I knew her intentions were good, but I was in the foggy in-between of grief and life anew.

Did I believe God gave Anderson Down syndrome? Or was Down syndrome a part of the new order we are all under in this fallen world—the conclusion I had clung to so adamantly when we first learned of his diagnosis? Even publicly.

On a blog I'd started a year before becoming pregnant with Anderson, I documented our wild year in Las Vegas. I named it *News Anchor to Homemaker*, complete with a perfect cartoon drawing of our family, me in a retro-style dress, Andy in his dress air force blues, and Violet dragging a news mic on the ground. My friend finished the new design just days before we received Anderson's final Down syndrome diagnosis. I knew the words I was writing didn't match the picture, nor did they match the life I felt slipping through my fingers, but I wrote them anyway, getting ahead of the story before it broke from another source.

September 30, 2014, blog excerpt:

Here is what we know: We know God did not intend for our son to have Down syndrome, just like God does not intend for people to get cancer. We know that God did not give us a son with Down syndrome because he believed we could handle it. We know that God would not test our faith by harming our child. We know that God would not punish us for our past sins by making our child go through this world with a life-altering condition. We know that we live in a fallen world where disease and disorders do not discriminate.

I had drawn a line in the sand. I didn't want anyone telling me their beliefs about why this happened to us, why this happened to him. No one was to cross my theology.

There was a problem with my theory, though, and thankfully the tide rolled in and erased the divide I'd spent weeks creating. I had assumed Down syndrome was a bad thing, and it would take months for my views to shift. It didn't happen all at once. It was a slow and steady climb. Because, again, when I received his diagnosis, I thought Down syndrome was an illness. It never occurred to me that Anderson's extra chromosome was an intrinsic part of his identity. It never occurred to me that God was the dance instructor. Back then I thought a different life meant a less-than life. I never wanted to be different. I always tried to fit the mold of what the world viewed as successful or even acceptable.

It never occurred to me that the seed planted in me so long ago was still affecting my views of not only God and the world but of myself and therefore of my unborn son.

I never slipped that tiny onesie over Anderson's head. Instead, I rolled it up and tucked it in the back of a drawer and for a time in the back of my mind. I didn't thank my mom for the gift, and we never spoke of it. Those beautiful, life-affirming words did not bring me rest as they do to so many. They brought me angst.

***

Parts of Psalm 139 are often quoted in ways to affirm a deterministic view of God—the belief that God intends everything that comes to pass. But it's important to consider the psalm from beginning to end. It begins with a declaration: "You have searched me, Lord, and you know me." The psalmist acknowledges he is known fully by God and from God. There is no escape.

In verse 6, he ends his first stanza with the recognition that although the Maker fully knows His creation, the created cannot fully know their Maker. "Such knowledge is too wonderful for me, too lofty for me to attain."

The psalm continues in verses 13–14 with the marveling of human formation: "For you created my inmost being; you knit me together in my mother's womb. I praise you because I am fearfully and wonderfully made."

And in verse 16, the psalmist goes on, saying, "All the days ordained for me were written in your book before one of them came to be."

The psalm takes a jarring turn at verse 19 and into verse 22, verses that are much less quoted: "If only you, God, would slay the wicked! . . . I have nothing but hatred for them; I count them my enemies."

The psalmist ends his prose in verse 24 with "See if there is any offensive way in me, and lead me in the way everlasting."

Scholars have a hard time classifying Psalm 139. Is it a prayer of thanksgiving? A plea? A defense? How do we reconcile its beautiful and often-quoted language alongside the hatred toward the psalmist's enemies? With certainty, he believes God was there from the beginning of his life, that God saw him as an embryo and knows him intimately now. He declares God already wrote out all his days and yet prays for Him to intervene in his written story. Amid his confidence in God's involvement in his life, he is also certain he does not fully know God or how He operates. There is tension in his wonder.

Old Testament scholar John Goldingay argues Psalm 139 is a prayer of confidence: "The emphasis lies on the fact that *you* know everything about *me* and that *you* are present everywhere that *I* am. It lies not on God's having predestined everything that happens to me or that I do but on the fact that *you* have set *my* destiny within your purpose."[1]

This feels right to me. God knows everything about us. He goes with us as we seek to discover Him, as we try to uncover the purposes He has for us here on earth.

But we can't know God's highest desires for us until we know ourselves, until we see ourselves as fearfully and wonderfully made. The process of life being created is so intricate, so detailed, so complex that we are living miracles. To think anything less is to have a small view of ourselves and in turn a small view of the One who made us.

You are the Divine's handiwork. The flecks of color in your eyes, the turn of your nose, the essence of your soul—God holds your unique identity. He expertly crafted you as the holy person you are and the holy person you are to become. He dreamt up the dream of you.

We were born out of love and made to carry this love with us throughout our lives. This love that created us lives in us, but it's not meant to just stay there. When we know we are loved by our creator and our love grows for Him, our love multiplies. Loving others is the natural outcome of being known. When we see ourselves as God's intentional, precious creations, we're also able to see others this way. Knowing ourselves as uniquely loved and knowing others as uniquely loved allows us to see God in it all, because He is present in all of us.

When we see ourselves and others as miracles, we're able to better know the miracle worker. Like the psalmist, I believe we can never fully know the ways of God. But we can recognize Him in us. We can recognize Him in one another. We can recognize that this mere breath that sinks in and out of our lungs is part of His intricate design. Such work, such wonder, can only be done on purpose.

This doesn't mean everything that happens to us happens on purpose, but that purpose is wired into our DNA. And we are to abide in this knowledge. We are to rest in knowing that our God is big enough to make us, every part of us, on purpose. He is that big, and we are that important to Him. Once this truth seeps into our bones, once it takes hold of our souls, the natural extension of this knowledge is to abound from it.

When we get up close to the tiny cells that make us who we are, we see God not as some far-off ruler but as our present creator. He created us, and He continues to do so, still. He gives us wisdom and wit and weaknesses too. It all adds up to the story of us, the story He's inviting us to write alongside Him. When we know our creator as existing in every fiber of our beings, we can write more boldly.

If someone gave Anderson a shirt now with the words "Fearfully and Wonderfully Made" across the front, I would no longer tuck it away in the back of a drawer. Back when he was still growing inside me, I unknowingly believed there was a human hierarchy, that there were the blessed and the unblessed. Now I believe in a God who is present in all His creations, from the tall cacti behind our old Alamogordo home, to the vast mountain range outside our Colorado home, to the joy alive in my son and in you.

Everywhere I look, God is there.

We are fearfully and wonderfully made because we are His and He is in us.

Walter Brueggemann suggests Hebrew wisdom literature may be one way to consider Psalm 139: "God created the world and life, and placed order in it, and God continues to sustain and govern that order. The task of humans is to seek and find that order and live into it."[2]

To seek and find seems like a lifelong mission.

God sees our unformed bodies and gives us our quirks, gifts, and special traits because He delights in us. Now it's time to seek and find who we are. Now it's time to seek and find what God desires for us. Now it's time to start living into our God-dreamed entirety.

The unexpected helps us return to who we were from the very beginning. The one God called *very good*.[3] We can trust Him on this. Our creator gave us instincts to listen to, not to ignore. He gave us talents to use, not to hide. His love for us is not scarce; it is vast. The Divine is big enough to wrap us and our unexpected moments within His love and within His purposes.

And His purposes are good.

Now that we're living vulnerably, now that we can see how society's version of success has corrupted our ideas of worth, now that we can zoom out and see what has shaped our ideas about God and about ourselves, we can emerge from the bathroom floor bare. The water that once hit us with our new reality has helped us return to ourselves—the ones God created. We can look in the mirror knowing we are intimately known and, here, loved just as we are. But we emerge from the waters once more knowing we aren't done yet, because God is not done with us.

I once thought my son with a disability needed healing, but I was the one who needed to be healed. I needed to be healed from the idea that I had to change myself in order to belong. I needed to be healed from the idea that worldly success and worth are tied together when in fact they are separate. I needed to be healed from the idea that God came here to punish, when really, He came here to restore.

Healing came when I realized that our identities are given to us by the One who makes and sustains all life. Once I realized a different life was not a less-than life, that my heart needed healing more than my son needed to be cured of atypicality, I was able to see myself more clearly. I was able to see my son more clearly too.

A 2011 study found that 99 percent of people with Down syndrome were happy with their lives.[4] Down syndrome isn't a mishap.

When we first received Anderson's diagnosis, I thought something was being taken away from him. I forgot it was an *extra* chromosome, that he was getting more. So were we.

> I once thought my son with a disability needed healing, but I was the one who needed to be healed.

I would soon discover my son is uniquely made and loved.

You are uniquely made and loved.

We are all uniquely made and loved.

And we are not done yet.

The unexpected helps us embrace our core selves. But, of course, we aren't meant to stay there. To live into our God-dreamed entirety, we must use our God-given uniqueness and our unexpected circumstances to impact the world in a way only we can. There will be push, and there will be pull. There will be steps forward and steps backward. The work of transformation is both challenging and beautiful.

Just as our very lives began, so they will continue with a dance.

- *Who was I then?*
  In the heat of the unexpected, how did I view uniqueness?

- *Who am I now?*
  What would working toward believing my neighbor and I are fearfully and wonderfully made look like, and how would it change me?

- *Who do I want to become?*
  Now that I'm doing the work of returning to my core self, how am I going to be free? What do I imagine living into my entirety would look like?

Part 2

The Gift of Unexpected Transformation

I do not understand the mystery of grace—only that it meets us where we are and does not leave us where it found us.

—Anne Lamott, *Traveling Mercies*

5

Letting Go

We were salivating over life's possibilities.

It was a Saturday morning in Las Vegas, during that short stretch of time after dental school and before we got the base assignment in Alamogordo. It was before Anderson was even a thought in our minds. Andy and I sat across from each other at my grandmother's hand-me-down kitchen table, still in our mismatched pajamas with a map and blank list between us. The air force needed dentists at nearly every base across the globe, making our choices endless.

Breakfast was over, but the smell of bacon still lingered. Baby Violet, not yet able to crawl, rolled around in the nearby sunroom, mouthing Sophie the Giraffe. I twirled my thick wavy hair into a bun, feeling distracted by its heaviness. I looked up at our white stucco-textured ceiling, hoping it somehow had the answer to Andy's question about which base to rank first.

"I want Italy," I said, "but I think our chances of getting Germany are higher, so let's rank it first." My words dripped with naïvety.

We filled out Andy's dream sheet of twenty locations with meticulous care. We penciled in mostly sought-after bases but sprinkled in more practical options so as to not appear greedy. We thought we knew the rules of a game only few know how to play. We thought with the right strategy, we would have a say in our military destiny.

Strategy had worked up to this point in our lives.

Life went pretty much as we planned our first four years of marriage. Not all the details, of course, but we'd mapped out our big stops and pulled into each one not too far off schedule. We thought we'd keep going down the path we'd drawn, it never dawning on us that we could go off course despite our hard work and careful tactics.

We thought life was linear.

We didn't know what was coming.

We never expected to like Nevada as much as we did. I cried when we first learned about our assignment. For two young adults who had grown up in the Southeast, we pictured a large sandpit littered with glowing neon.

This was not on the map we'd drawn for our lives.

We didn't know Vegas is home to gorgeous silver mountains and dotted with palm trees. We didn't know the red rocks would sing to us like the beaches back home in Florida and Georgia. We also didn't know it was within driving distance of some of the country's most prized possessions, its national parks, preserves, and monuments.

We were thankful for the United States' many federal holidays and took advantage of every three-day weekend. We became traveling pros and armed our car with road-trip parenting essentials: Baby Einstein DVDs, snack puffs, and pre-mixed formula. We were fueled by Starbucks sugary lattes, freedom, and a desire to be swept away by a life turning out to be bigger than we'd imagined. We hiked Zion's famous trails, got up close to Bryce's deep orange hoodoos, and rang in the new year overlooking the Grand Canyon.

We didn't know the beauty of the unexpected until we found ourselves in its territory. As holiday time off approached, I'd usher Violet off to her afternoon nap and open my laptop to lands of possibilities.

We woke up in a hotel room overlooking Utah's Lake Powell on Easter morning. With no family around, we'd decided to spend the most sacred day of the year in one of God's most spectacular creations—Antelope Canyon. The sun was just beginning to illuminate the grand tan rock formations outside our window when Violet made it clear she wanted out of her travel crib. I took a deep breath and pushed back the curtains to take in the peachy morning glow, then lifted my daughter's newly turned one-year-old body out of her bed and shuffled my feet across the scratchy industrial carpet to place her next to Andy.

We didn't know the beauty of the unexpected until we found ourselves in its territory.

I started preparing coffee in the small hotel brewer, pouring the dark grains into a flower-shaped filter. As hot water dripped into the glass pot, an old hymn began flowing through my mind. My diaphragm expanded across my skin, and I started singing in our church of three—*He lives!*

Andy walked over, wrapped his arm around my waist, and said "I love when you sing" before kissing the back of my neck.

Before we set out for the day, we made a picnic breakfast on the white plastic-slatted chairs by the hotel pool. Our makeshift table overlooked Glen Canyon. The lumpy tan and brown rocks looked prehistoric and were mirrored by the still, glass-like lake below. I'm not sure if it was because of Easter, that sight, or both, but the morning felt draped in holiness. My second cup of coffee was filled to the brim, and I was full of a peace I hadn't known in some time.

As I gazed at the quiet lake in front of us, the Easter peace flowed through my veins and out my mouth. "No matter which base we get, it will be good," I said while eating one of our mass-produced breakfast sandwiches. I handed Violet a strawberry from my fruit cup, which she took with her still-dimpled fist.

Andy looked at me the way he does when he's feeling completely in love.

"I know it," I added with confidence.

Our Vegas year showed us a world outside of work, a world I was open to exploring further. We kept that in mind when we filled out our dream sheet. The only bases we listed without TV stations were overseas. Only extreme adventures would lock that door and discard the key.

He lives, after all. I had only just met Him, and I thought to claim Him meant a hedge of protection was now around me. Everything would work out just as it should, because He lives.

I finished the last bit of coffee. It was lukewarm.

When breakfast was over, we set out for Antelope Canyon, formed by years of flash floods tearing through sandstone and strong winds whipping around grains of sand. Years of destruction resulted in the stunning underground museum filled with canvases painted with orange and red swirls.[1]

As we stepped into the slot canyon and made our way through halls the color of earth and fire, I never thought about the destruction that produced the wonder surrounding us. Though we were underground, heaven poured through openings above. The sunlight highlighted each crevice.

I didn't know every detail above, and below was a scar with a story to tell.

That Easter morning, I saw only the result, the beauty right before me. At that time in my life, I was one to skip over the horror of Good Friday, the confusion of Holy Saturday, and land right at the resurrection.

We revere the cross, but we don't want to sit under its weight for too long. We don't want to feel the forsakenness our God felt. We want Him ascending from a mountaintop.

And we miss the fullness of the miracle.

Just like we sometimes skip over the surprise pain of the cross, I ignored the land's unexpected story. I focused only on the outcome, and I missed the lesson in front of me—death is required for resurrection.

Photographers from around the world make the trek to this remote part of Navajo Nation to capture Antelope's unmatched splendor. We only had our fifth-generation iPhones, but we didn't care.

We were wrapped in certainty.

Life was beautiful and would continue to be.

We'd been waiting for May 8, 2014, for almost a year—the day we'd learn where the air force was sending us next. I felt like a kid on Christmas morning, but instead of wrapped presents waiting under a tree, the next three to four years of our lives were wrapped in a phone call. I had visions of Europe, California, and Washington State dancing in my head, each presenting different fates—all of them good, some of them glamorous. My phone was practically glued to my hand despite the nervous sweat. I waited, I paced, and finally, a ring. It was Andy.

Quick. Wipe off damp finger. Swipe.

"What did we get?" I gasped.

"Holloman Air Force Base," he said.

Silence.

"Andy . . . where is that?"

"Alamogordo, New Mexico."

Oh, God.

In the list of twenty bases we ranked that Saturday morning six months earlier, this was on the small list of five worst-case scenarios—not on the dream sheet. The worst-case scenario bases were not only undesirable but also so remote there was no option for me to go back to TV news. This was it. This was the doomed ledge I talked myself down from when the Easter peace ran dry.

Possibilities of an adventure, career, or both crumbled with a thirty-second phone call. I called my mom and cried. Then I hung up and cried some more. I felt guilty as Violet crawled around me. She looked at me with her big blue eyes as my own would not stop leaking. My career was over, and so were the life scenarios Andy and I had dreamed up over glasses of cheap wine and late-night chats. I cried so much that the whites of my eyes turned red, making my irises appear an eerie shade of see-through aqua.

I was devastated. How could this happen? How could the worst-case scenario be *my* life? This was not on the map.

The year 2013 had been a gift. After four years of Andy's intense schooling and my out-of-the-ordinary job, we'd needed rest. It was the first time we each had time to nurture our relationship. Instead of measuring who was contributing more around the house, we saw each other, were grateful for each other. We delighted in *us*. Our marriage blossomed in those calendar pages.

I had made a mistake thinking life would keep going this way. I thought after years of hard work and empty bank accounts, we were full and would never be empty again. I couldn't have known that 2013 was a foundation-builder for everything to come. Plans would be drawn and redrawn, our only normal the constant stretching of expectations and abandonment of long-held notions, a continual filling and emptying. Life was about to unravel, and in the unraveling, we would hold on to each other tighter than we ever had.

My white T-shirt had black mascara stains scattered across the front. I curled up in my old floral chair, feeling as blue as the flowers stretched across its surface. I felt tricked—by myself, by God. *I really thought it was going to be good news.* In the middle of my muddled thoughts, I also felt a nudge telling me to take a pregnancy test. We hadn't been trying to get pregnant, but after Decaf Coffee Night . . .

I had an old test tucked away in a bathroom drawer from the first go-around. It had somehow made the cross-country move, and I felt it calling. But I also didn't trust myself, my emotions. Taking it felt self-destructive.

How will a negative test make me feel right now? Why are you doing this? I argued with myself, but the nudge turned into a push.

I hung my head in my hands as I waited for the result, believing it would be negative, knowing I'd set myself up for extra heartbreak over something I wasn't even planning on being mine.

My sight was still blurry from the tears, but when I lifted my eyes, the message on the digital screen was clear—PREGNANT. I slapped my forehead in shock. While my skin still tingled, I took the test to better lighting, snapped a photo, and sent it to my mom. Then I lay on the carpet in our sunroom and laughed and cried at the same time.

I thanked God. *You knew I needed this news today. You want me to be a stay-at-home-mom. This is all part of your perfect plan.*

That Easter peace was not deceiving; I was not duped. The news really was going to be good. Our lives were still good. *He* was still good.

He lives.

I was new to blogging and had just learned how to make graphics. I took a photo of the test next to a map I printed of New Mexico, uploaded the image to a digital editor, and typed in bold print, *God's Perfect Plan*. Andy walked in the door defeated, but I was armed with a piece of paper declaring good news. This wasn't one of the planned stops on our map but one our creator wrote in before we ever met.

I set up my phone to record me revealing the surprise to Andy. We would want to relive this moment—the moment our story moved from defeat to hope—for years to come.

Andy opened the paper I'd carefully crafted, then looked at me and said, "Oh, you're kidding."

He threw his head back and laughed, and then his laughter turned to tears accompanied by deep breathy gasps. I turned off the recording and cried some more.

God did not forsake us. This assignment was big and unexpected, but our lives were not shattered.

I had it all figured out.

I'm convinced New Mexico holds both the ugliest and most beautiful scenery in the United States. But we'd lived in the Las Vegas desert for a year, and I was just beginning to see how the opposites are often intertwined. The unsightly vegetation of the desert floor, the sand and twisted shrubs, make the mountains pop with more glory.

When we caravanned into Alamogordo for the first time, we saw a gorgeous dark-green mountain range dotted with layers of rocky jewels, but instead of cactus blooms at its base there was one long stretch of fast-food restaurants. Red and yellow plastic signs littered the skyline one after the other, packed in tight like a line of dominoes.

My stomach tumbled. I'm still not sure why a town with only thirty thousand residents needs two Sonics on the same road, but apparently, the people of Alamogordo can't get enough limeades.

We passed the one grocery store in town on our left and took a right off the main road, onto the other road that makes up Alamogordo. As with most military towns, the scenery grew worse the closer we got to base. Highway 70 is one long stretch of power lines and billboards. We passed junkyards, a run-down motel, and an adult video store on the left. On the right was a used car dealership and a German restaurant housed in a narrow warehouse. At least it was local.

Base was thankfully familiar with guards at the gate and airplanes on display. We decided to eat at the BX for lunch, putting a fence between us and our new town. It doesn't matter which base you visit, the food court is always the same, complete with some restaurants I was sure the rest of the world had stopped frequenting in the '90s. We chose a table with a view of the mountain range we passed while driving in, trying to stare at the positive in front of us, willing it to seep into our minds.

Andy broke the silence. "We're going to rock this."

His words made me burst into tears over my O'Charley's sub. He'd just affirmed what I was thinking—it was as bad as we first imagined.

Homes are surprisingly expensive in Alamogordo. The German air force has a unit stationed at Holloman, and the Deutsche officers have a much higher housing allowance, which drives up rental prices. *Wilkommen!* was on every property sign. Andy's captain rank plus specialty pay didn't quite make the cut on the type of home we could afford in Las Vegas.

The house we ended up living in on Cherry Hills Loop was outdated and overpriced. It had cheap laminate and tile more than twenty years old. The layout was choppy, and the electric stovetop left me wanting. But it was sturdy. It was also the house where our lives as we knew them ended and then slowly began again, changed. The walls held our tears, our confusion, and perhaps for the first time in our lives, our uncertainty.

——— The Gift ———

Blueprints were widely used in construction for over a century. When architects or engineers finalized their plans for a building project, they transferred their drawing onto a blueprint for reproduction. The blueprint birthed every part of a new structure. From its measurements and angles, workers poured the foundation, erected beams, and wired electricity. The image itself took several steps to construct. The creators drew the plan on cartridge paper, then traced the project on tracing paper, then clamped the tracing paper in a daylight exposure frame where ultraviolet light transmitted through the sheet and the light-sensitive coating converted the image to a dark blue.

The process was so exact that it made the project difficult to change. With digital advancements, blueprints are rarely used today, but the name stuck. A blueprint, simply put, is a detailed plan.

Author and historian Kate Bowler says the unexpected often leaves us asking three questions:

Why?

God, are you here?

What does this suffering mean?

She said that, at first, in her own unexpected cancer diagnosis, these questions "had enormous weight and urgency."[2]

I know this to be true.

My biggest questions in the early days of Anderson's diagnosis—the questions that inspired the first version of this book—were these:

Is Down syndrome in God's blueprint for Anderson's life?

Is parenting a child with Down syndrome in the blueprint of my own?

Is there a blueprint at all?

I even enrolled in seminary hoping to find the answers.

In an apologetics class, we studied different theodicies—arguments that attempt to explain how a good God and evil can coexist. I considered theologian John Hick's argument that evil is necessary for humans to become who God intends them to be; Augustine's aesthetic beauty theodicy, where evil makes us see God's goodness more clearly; and professor and apologist William Edgar's deterministic view that God didn't create evil but ordains all that comes to pass—therefore using evil now that it's here.[3]

I also considered religion philosopher Alvin Plantinga's free-will defense, which concludes evil exists because of human's misuse of their God-given freedom.[4] I held on tightly to the last one, and I am admittedly coming to you with a skew toward that perspective.

But really, I recognize some truth in all of them. And really, I have to let go of the certainty I was once desperate to find. Because God, His plans, His ways cannot be fully known.

I don't think for God to be sovereign means everything that happens is His ideal will. I don't believe the God of love needs to divvy out a certain number of diseases, accidents, or heart defects in order to fulfill some unseen higher purpose. I don't credit God for tragedies that break our hearts and His.[5]

But I have seen truths from these theologians' arguments. I know the unexpected, even the truly heartbreaking things I have experienced outside of this book, have helped my becoming.

I've experienced how facing something life-altering and per-manent can hurt for a time, but with time, end up making our existence more beautiful. I've seen how God uses pain that comes from evil in this world and bends it toward something good.

The closest thing I feel to certainty about God is that He is love and is purposefully mysterious. Through all the question-ing and studying, I have come to know this: Our creator is not a fact to learn but a presence to realize. I have grown closer to God in the cycle of catching and releasing, realizing I will never have a corner on His truth.

We will inevitably come up short if we try to explain why pain exists, because God chose not to explain its complexity to us. But what I've come to believe is that it's possible that God, though He has good hopes for each of us, allows things to happen outside of His ideal will in the name of freedom.

In circumstances we wouldn't choose, and perhaps God would not choose for us, He miraculously makes blessings come out of brokenness. In the absence of answers, there is comfort in the One who left a perfect home to live in this one. When uncertainty feels heavy, relief is in the One who not only sees our pain but intimately knows its weight.

God used people to tell His story, but there are holes in the book. That's why so many Christian denominations with different sets of beliefs about what is God-willed and what is not exist. God didn't leave us a blueprint for our faith—and I believe purposefully so. He would have had to control the messengers and the message.

Jesus came to give us the most accurate picture of God with-out stripping away our choice. God is love, and He always was. Through Jesus, we get the greatest depiction of who we belong to. Jesus liberated the image we had of God, and in doing so, He liberated us all.

God loves us enough to not give us all the answers, because in doing so He would be forcing us into Him.

God does not control. He loves.

⁓

What was called a blueprint years ago is now just called a drawing. It's a crucial first step in the building process—pricing, logistics, and site planning all come from the drawing. But unlike the old blueprints, the drawing is flexible. When the project breaks ground, contractors inevitably hit bumps, and when they do, they make changes called redlines. These additional lines to the drawing are where changes had to be made to adapt to the unexpected. When the beams are erected, the walls put in place, and the last shingle laid, the contractor crafts a revised document called an as-built.

Perhaps the things unexpected to us weren't in the original drawings of our lives. Perhaps they're unforeseen factors that came up later in the building process, and it's our job to embrace the redline and support the new element. Perhaps a drawing is a more accurate picture of how life is for all of us. Maybe we are the contractors working off the master engineer's vision of our lives. When the unexpected forces us to go off plan, we have the liberty to decide how we'll move forward.

We hope we do our best to keep building well, to keep building in the image the Creator wants for us. And at the end of our assignment, we hand the owner the revised document and hope we feel proud of the final product—and so does He.

⁓

During our short time in Alamogordo, we mostly stayed inside our little house on Cherry Hills Loop. But when we ventured out, it was often to the same place—White Sands National Monument, the bright spot of Alamogordo.

Not too far from where the government tested the first atomic bomb is this natural wonder where miles of cold white sands peak and valley below the backdrop of dark gray mountains, which appear almost blue at certain points of the day.

Thousands of years ago, Lake Otero covered this part of New Mexico. Forces of nature swept the water away, leaving only salt and gypsum behind. Over time, gusts of desert winds broke down the gypsum into the small grains still there today.[6]

It took losing what once was to birth the beauty that now is.

Sometimes it takes losing what is to birth the beauty of what will be.

So many of those stunning places we traveled to during our year in Vegas, our time before the unexpected—like the Grand Canyon and Antelope Canyon—are products of destruction. This message is laced throughout nature. From the tiniest caterpillar that must turn into goo inside a cocoon before it can sprout butterfly wings, to the earth crashing against itself to form mountain peaks, God gives beauty for ashes.

Sometimes it takes losing what is to birth the beauty of what will be.

Once we let go of the *why* our lives have been shattered, once we let go of the need for certainty, once we let go of the idea that life is linear—a route we can neatly follow along a map—we can move forward ready to endure the devastating and beautiful process of transformation.

Author Sarah Bessey writes, "The times in my life when I have experienced transformation, it has been at the intersection of my choices and the divine."[7]

I pray we can meet at this intersection. There's a time for questions and a time to lay the questions down. There's a time to pursue and a time to surrender. He makes everything beautiful in His time.[8] But we have to walk to this point where we surrender to the mystery, undergo the pressure of change, and ask it to help us live into the fullness of ourselves.

We come to this point holding the complexity with open hearts. We release our need for certainty, let go of the map we envisioned our lives would follow, and begin to trust God to work through our unexpected moments by breaking through. He broke through the veil of heaven and entered earth. He breaks through still.

Whether or not God is the force behind the destruction, He will break through here. He *is* here. But we have to be willing to undergo this force, the drying up of something we once had, the whipping winds, and believe He will use it all to create something new out of us. One day we will stand atop this new creation and let the cold sand run through our fingers and marvel at His work. We have a God who resurrected from death. He resurrects still.

One day, after weeks had passed since the amniocentesis results, I sat atop one of those chilled dunes and watched Violet gingerly toddle in her hot-pink sneakers that almost glowed against the white sand. Later, I snapped a photo of Andy carrying her on his shoulders with the bright gypsum beneath his feet and the tall mountains off in the distance. I had felt so empty despite the new life growing inside me. But here on this mountain made of sand, both firm and delicate, the light was peeking through the darkness. I could see life was beautiful now and that perhaps a new kind of beauty was coming.

I was not at the intersection, but I was getting closer.

One day, I would arrive.

I believe one day you will too.

It requires pursuing and letting go, sometimes in and out and over again.

Life is paradoxical.

Transformation is too.

Beauty and destruction are not always opposites but often intertwine.

Beauty can come.

And beauty is here.

THE *Gift* OF *You*

- *Who was I then?*
  What did I believe with such certainty that was dashed
  once the unexpected hit, and how did this affect me?

- *Who am I now?*
  Do I still feel certainty is necessary? And if so, why? What
  quest for certainties do I need to let go?

- *Who do I want to become?*
  How can I live in the tension with open hands? How can
  I move forward with hope in a God who brings forth new
  and beautiful things out of destruction?

6

Becoming Real

In the soupy period after receiving the amniocentesis results, there was no division between days. Sadness was interlaced with responsibilities. I checked off the boxes that needed to be checked each day, but grief hung in the air, creating a thick haze. It was all I could do not to choke on the fumes.

One afternoon I walked by our wedding portrait, and I stopped and studied it for the first time in years. Andy has his back against a tall pine. He's pulling my waist against his, our lips just barely touch, and a vineyard is below us and an extravagant chateau is behind us. We are surrounded by green. Life was a plot of good soil waiting for us to plant and reap our dreams. The photo is full of possibilities.

Looking at it, my eyes filled with water. The sad face reflecting back at me in the portrait glass didn't fit. We were supposed to have a beautiful life. I had no idea it would end like this. This felt like an ending, an end to the life robbed from us, an end to the life we felt entitled to, an end to the happy-ever-after we thought we were promised.

I thought beauty was behind us.

I didn't know what was ahead.

We had to move away from Alamogordo because the remote air force base couldn't handle our unborn baby's needs. We filled out another dream sheet with options all near family on the East Coast, but once again, we got nothing on our list. We were heading even farther from home, farther west, to Tucson, Arizona.

We would be parenting a child with a disability alone.

No village.

We would have to figure out this new life together, just Andy and me.

We lived in the New Mexico desert for only three-and-a-half months. Most of our belongings weren't even unpacked long enough to collect a layer of dust, and yet so much life happened there. The weeks had never moved so quickly or so slowly. The changes were sweeping, and yet the minutes crawled. When I look back at our time living in the house on Cherry Hills Loop, it seems as if years played out inside its walls.

That's because Alamogordo holds our before-and-after moment.

It came with the words *Your baby has Down syndrome*, and in the days that followed, we were mourning and transforming. We still had this privileged idea of how the world worked and how it should work, a world that had mostly worked for us up to that point.

Then our before-and-after moment dashed our faith and started building a new one. The foundation was the same, but the ideas and certainties we'd constructed on top were being stripped away even when we didn't quite recognize it yet. We could never go back to the time before the doctor uttered those words.

Life would never be the same as before we stepped over the threshold on Cherry Hills Loop.

We would never be the same once we left it.

It was early afternoon and particularly dusty out when we drove away from Alamogordo. I refused to look in the rearview mirror, feeling poetic about it all.

Maybe this is a bad chapter we can finally close.

We were praying for healing. We thought Anderson needed to be healed of his intellectual disability. We would soon discover that we were the ones who needed to be healed of our intellectual certainties.

We knew the amniocentesis had given us a sure diagnosis, but we believed God could still heal our son. Maybe in this next chapter, He would. Maybe we would get a yes to this most important prayer. With imaginary scales, we envisioned balancing the world's blessings and hardships. We thought we were due to toss a pebble onto the winning side.

By the time most of the empty moving boxes had been taken to the Tucson dump and curtains were once again hung, my due date was only a month away. So while Andy was at his new dental clinic and I was settling into our new house with my swollen feet propped up, I started prepping. Two months prior, I had joined an online pregnancy support group through the Down Syndrome Diagnosis Network. Little by little, my perspective started shifting. At first, I thought the women in the group were trying to spin our terrible fates into a tapestry woven with manufactured positivity. I thought they were fooling themselves and fooling me.

But I stuck around. And in those final weeks of my pregnancy, among virtual strangers, my grief became hope. Only it was not hope that our son would be cured; it was hope for his future if he remained exactly the same. I found myself cracking the spines of books and pouring over articles. Although I was still scared, I began to feel cautiously excited for this new life—not just a new baby but a baby with Down syndrome.

But if I allowed myself to feel hopeful, joyful even, was I giving up on God healing him? I felt torn, guilty, and I didn't know what to pray for anymore.

The epidural numbed me physically, but my heart felt everything as I watched the clock strike midnight. Our son would be born on December 31, 2014.

Call it mother's intuition, or the Holy Spirit, but I'd predicted our son would be born on New Year's Eve despite his due date being almost two weeks later.

Two weeks earlier, Andy and I had just finished eating scoops of frozen custard on an ideal Arizona winter night. We were alone in the car, making our way toward the east side of Tucson to our new house that still didn't feel like ours.

"Choose a date. When do you think he'll be born?" Andy asked me.

"New Year's Eve," I said without hesitation.

"Why do you think the thirty-first?"

"Because I think God will show us a miracle on the last day of the worst year of our lives." After two unwelcome moves and an unwanted diagnosis, I thought it would be God's way of redeeming 2014.

Now in the glow of the chirping hospital monitors, I felt mesmerized, believing our creator was in the room. He was showing us we had not slipped through His fingers. He was holding us through the details.

Andy fell asleep on the plastic couch, but I couldn't rest. Although I felt torn over praying for healing, I thought I should give it one last shot. I got out my pen and wrote a plea.

But as I poured out my thoughts on those pages, my words were coming up short. They were forced. My heart wasn't behind them. I knew it was God's way of telling me He had answered this prayer we'd been praying for months with no. His way of telling me I didn't even want the answer to be yes anymore. I was ready for this new life to begin—for my new life to begin too.

I put down my pen and closed my eyes knowing I could stop my plea.

My eyes weren't shut for long. This epidural wasn't as effective as the one I had with my first delivery.

For months, I had lived in pain. Like contractions, the pain would sometimes come in small spurts and other times all at once with such intensity that I couldn't talk, walk, or do anything through it. I had no choice but to surrender and sit under its power. But I didn't want to feel this pain now if I didn't have to.

I called the nurse in and told her the epidural wasn't working and something was wrong. She was young and new to labor and delivery. I'm sure she thought I was being dramatic since she'd just checked me thirty minutes earlier, but I persuaded her to check again.

I had gone from 6 to 10 centimeters.

I woke Andy, and seconds later the delivery and NICU teams piled into our still-dark room. Andy held my hand as I pushed. For five minutes, I gave it my all, and in the dawn of New Year's Eve, at exactly five a.m., the child we had prayed and mourned over exited the house I once felt failed him and entered the world.

He didn't cry.

I asked if he was okay over and over again, the way mothers do during dramatic birth scenes in movies. I saw the doctor holding up our son's small frame across the room, his little body looking so heavy. Unlike Violet, who had kicked and screamed her way into life, he just hung there midair. The team jumped in to do their assessments as I lay in bed helpless, watching as Andy snapped a few photos.

Finally, a nurse bundled up our baby and put him in my arms. My husband—his father—stood beside us.

Andy and I looked at our son, looked at each other, and knew. The answer to any remaining question was in his eyes. His dark almond-shaped eyes stared into mine so deeply that they broke through.

He broke through and found me.

And I, him.

A miracle.

The thing we feared, Down syndrome, was here, and it was beautifully bound in a six-pound baby boy—our baby.

"What's his name?" the doctor asked us.

"Anderson," we said in unison.

For the first time in months, waves of peace washed over me. The umbilical cord had been cut, but this moment was when I finally felt connected to the boy who knew me from within. Anderson wasn't a mishap of nature or a statistic; he was a baby with a dainty button nose, his sister's chin, and a strong gaze that seemed to be drinking us in.

The thing we feared, Down syndrome, was here, and it was beautifully bound in a baby boy—our baby.

His life had been so noisy inside me—crying parents, moving trucks, constant ultrasound wands intruding his space. Together, the three of us welcomed the quiet.

When the last of the delivery team finally cleared, I said to Andy, "I feel like you need to put your head on my shoulder and cry." And he did.

We didn't speak. We didn't need to because I knew what he was feeling. It was the end of the four worst months of our lives. It was every emotion at once. It was joy and sadness. It was peace of the now known and fear of the unknowns that lingered. I had been processing for months, but Andy couldn't until his son was born.

The three of us sat there in the early morning hours holding on to one another. There, love grew. Salty tears were salves to wounds opened by the unexpected. Wrapped in each other's arms, in the glow of New Year's Eve, healing began.

Before moving on, Andy needed to feel everything the way I had on the bathroom floor after the amniocentesis results. And he did so quickly because something wasn't right with Anderson. I thought something was off from the moment he came out. Despite his strong gaze, he seemed too lethargic. When a nurse came back into our room, she noticed it too. She ran a quick test, discovered low oxygen levels, and off to the NICU our baby went.

Andy went into protector mode. He calmly asked the doctors questions and put their answers into a language I could understand. He was either at my side or Anderson's side, comforting us both.

Family trickled in, and surprisingly, for the first time in years, so did flurries of a rare southern Arizona snow. Tears were cried, smiles were curled, laughter came back into our lives by the tiny crib side of the intensive care unit. We oohed and aahed over Anderson's hair, and we fussed over the nasal cannula giving him oxygen. He was getting stronger, and so were we.

Some fears were already proving to be unfounded. The fear of feeling disappointed when seeing Down syndrome faded at the first glimpse of his face. But now, as I looked at his small chest moving up and down, up and down with tangled wires following the rhythm, I knew some of my fears were valid.

Two days after he was born, I took one step into Anderson's barren nursery and melted into a puddle on the laminate floor. The walls were decorated with vintage airplanes, the crib was dressed, but there was no baby to rest inside. Anderson had to stay in the NICU because of his low oxygen levels. I knew it was a possibility; I had seen enough babies with Down syndrome on the internet to know NICU stays were common. But crossing the threshold of his room with empty arms made the heaviness that had engulfed me for months return. The pregnancy chapter, with its waiting and wondering, was over, but the new chapter was on hold.

As hard as it was initially, I grew accustomed to my baby being at the hospital. I visited the hard and went home to the life I knew before. I got scared about his full integration into our daily lives. I wanted life with our son to begin, but I found comfort in the distance between us and unknowns that came with his disability. The distance created space for old fears to settle back in.

Healing had taken place over the weeks leading up to Anderson's arrival. And the day he was born, a thin coat of tissue finally appeared, binding the gash of the unexpected. But the first layer of repair was fresh and fragile. Wounds sometimes have a way of reopening.

Boom-boom.

Growing up near the Kennedy Space Center, you knew when it was a shuttle launch day. If you ever missed the announcement in the paper or on TV, you were quickly reminded by the outsiders. Tourists swarmed our usually quiet town, and if the launch was scrubbed, they hung around until it was *all systems go*. Our normally near-empty streets were littered with cars bearing license plates from states near and far. People from all over the world set up lawn chairs on the side of U.S. Route 1 and in abandoned parking lots, all to catch a glimpse of the man-made wonder.

But while anticipation was always high on launch day, landing day was a different story. The mission's ending wasn't nearly as exciting as its beginning. As a kid, the only way I knew it was landing day was from hearing the *boom-boom*. Sonic booms were a routine part of life for us. When a space shuttle reentered the earth, only miles away from our town, its arrival created a pause in the day or woke us in the night.

The double explosion–type sound was caused by shock waves. The space shuttle created those waves upon reentering the earth, traveling faster through the air than the speed of sound. Sonic booms are an aftershock.

After a week in the NICU, Anderson came home. With low muscle tone, and now a confirmed hole in his heart, he took nearly an hour to drink each of his eight bottles a day. Between pumping and feeding, his calorie consumption alone was a full-time job.

I'd read about the therapists and specialists he would need to see during his first year, but I didn't realize how quickly our day-to-day life would revolve around medical appointments. In the mess of transitioning from one child to two, in the reality of a disability introduced to our family, life was again unrecognizable.

For weeks, I lived in the aftershock. The preparation, the grief, the research, the hope had all launched me to this place. The first part of the mission was complete, and now there was no crowd to cheer me on as I rolled along the landing strip.

Because we were new in town, there was no crowd at all. I was alone and living in one big sonic boom, the shockwaves of re-entering life traveling faster than I could keep up with.

Boom-boom.

It was late February. Violet and Anderson woke up from their morning naps, and I got them ready to meet Andy for lunch. He greeted us in the parking lot, his smile stretched all the way across his face the way it used to, making the wrinkles around his eyes more prominent. He was floating on air, and I was gasping for it.

I told him in a not-so-subtle way that my life was miserable. "My life is miserable" is what I said over our plates of fries.

I knew my words would wipe the old familiar smile off his face, but I couldn't hold them back. I didn't want to. I needed him to know how bad off I was. He got to leave home for the day. He got to have conversations with adults. He got to think of things other than developmental charts, scary medical conversations, and dirty diapers. He got to escape our reality. But I was consumed with it. Every feeding, every doctor's appointment, every therapy session was a reminder of how far life had gone off course.

I had thought the darkest days were behind me. I thought the chapter should have closed by now. Instead, I found myself in a new chapter with similar pages, where grief hung in the dry air.

We had moved out of one desert into another, but it was still a desert. I had no friends and no time to make them with all of Anderson's health concerns. Isolation is a breeding ground for resentment, and I was pregnant with bitterness. I was by myself, carrying a load I could not handle on my own, parched and in need of water.

The Gift

When Andy and I were in the nine-month Bible study two years earlier, I couldn't wait to get to Psalms. After trudging through the Old Testament laws, I wanted to feel inspired. I wanted to feel light. I didn't know that more than half of the Psalms are laments. When my life was happy, I couldn't help but feel disappointed by the somber words staring back at me.

I didn't know the Psalms were showing me the scope of what it means to be fully human and fully loved.

In his book *Spirituality of the Psalms*, Walter Brueggemann breaks the Psalms into three categories: orientation, disorientation, and new orientation.

The psalms of orientation are when the writer's life is in a season of satisfaction—the writer is filled with gratitude, and his words reflect the goodness of God.

The psalms of disorientation are when the writer is in a season of suffering—the language reflects the painful disarray the psalmist is in, at times using hyperbole to express the depth of his anguish.

The psalms of new orientation are when the light finally breaks through the darkness the writer was once consumed by—joy has come again.

As I mentioned in the introduction to this book, Western Christian culture would have us believe there's a short pain arc when we experience the unexpected and that we should rush to the bright side as quickly as possible. But the Psalms show us that bringing our whole selves to God is foundational to being in a relationship with Him.

Dr. Brueggemann explains this further:

The complaints of various kinds, the cries for vengeance and profound penitence are foundational to a life of faith in this

116

particular God. Much Christian piety and spirituality is romantic and unreal in its positiveness. As children of the Enlightenment, we have censored and selected around the voice of darkness and disorientation, seeking to go from strength to strength, from victory to victory. But such a way not only ignores the Psalms; it is a lie in terms of our experience. Brevard S. Childs is no doubt right in seeing that the Psalms as a canonical book is finally an act of hope. But the hope is rooted precisely in the midst of loss and darkness, where God is surprisingly present.[1]

The Psalms do not allow us to ignore the darkness. But thank God, He is surprisingly there. I believe this is why Jesus quoted a psalm on the cross: "My God, my God, why have you forsaken me?"[2]

In His darkest hour, Jesus showed us "relentless solidarity."[3]

I know what it's like to be human.

I know what it's like to feel pain.

I know what it's like to feel the absence of God.

I know.

And I know this isn't the end.

The Psalms are countercultural because we aren't meant to skip over the darkness but to enter it. We're meant to find God there.

When we let go of the pressure—the desire, even—to go from positive to positive, we're living within the fullness of our humanity. We have to break up with the toxic positivity that permeates our culture in order to learn a new way—the way of being known.

And this new way gives us a new way of knowing.

This is how we become real—with ourselves and the One who made us.

This is how we undergo the unexpected.

News of Anderson's diagnosis and then the aftershock of his birth were the first times I really sat in the darkness. The days were long and incredibly hard. Transitioning to two kids is difficult, but adding in a new town where I didn't know anyone and the real medical issues Anderson was facing, to not feel the effects of darkness would have been to not feel at all.

> **The Psalms are countercultural because we aren't meant to skip over the darkness but to enter it. We're meant to find God there.**

But I didn't know it at the time. My grief made me feel guilty. I bought into the lie sold by Western Christianity. The lie that says our pain has a beginning, middle, and end. The lie that says it's our job to get to the end as quickly as possible. The lie that says it's our job to be the best PR staff for our religion, to focus only on the light and ignore the dark.

But like life, pain isn't linear. It doesn't follow a predetermined timeline. On the day Anderson was born, I naïvely thought the peace I felt in the glow of the hospital monitors would be permanent.

In my search for lightness, I missed the message of what it means to be human and in relationship with this God—that the way *to* is *through*. I thought I was turning my back on God, but instead, I was unknowingly drawing closer to Him. He was in the darkness with me even when I could not see. He used the inevitable darkness of this time to start transforming me.

He met me there.

He will meet you there in the darkness too. He will set this holy work into motion in the depths of your soul. But you have to be willing to sit with Him.

Psalms tells a story of grief and then hope. Psalm 13:1–3 says, "How long, LORD? Will you forget me forever? . . . Look on me and answer, LORD my God. Give light to my eyes, or

I will sleep in death." But the psalm ends with this, in verses 5 and 6: "But I trust in your unfailing love . . . I will sing the LORD's praise, for he has been good to me."

The way we get to this transforming hope, the way we find our way out of the darkness, is by giving our all over to God.

It was through the wrestling with the shadows, by finally being real with myself and real with Him, that I was able to see the light when I was ready. Shadows only exist because somewhere a light is present.

And one day the rays filled the dark hole I was in. It didn't come through the form of a new friend or a new revelation. It was him. It was Anderson. At ten weeks old, he smiled his first real smile. With each upward turn of his lips, the hardness of my heart began to crumble, and what was left began to change. Like his dad, Anderson smiled with his whole face, leaving me no option but to smile back with all of mine. The smiles became frequent, and soon they were accompanied by laughs and a repetition of "a-goos" he said with such gusto. He was sweet, quick with a giggle, and rarely complained despite all the pokes and prods from doctors. His smiles allowed me to see him for the first time all over again, like a second birth.

God used Anderson to bring me out of the hole. He took my hand and showed me the beauty of the desert floor, and the unruly shrubs atop the sand were sprouting blooms I had never seen. He showed me who Anderson was and gave me a glimpse of who he might become. He showed me Anderson's life was beautiful—and so was mine.

I believe God used Anderson to bring me to this transforming hope. I don't know if I would have recognized it if I hadn't let myself feel the effects of the aftershock. As I unburdened my heart, a channel opened. There he was, ready for me with a smile.

Just as it is with the roots of trees that bring us life with their fruit, or the plants of the field that create the air we breathe, so, too, our growth is rooted in the darkness where God is not absent but there, helping us grow, helping us live into our entireties.

A few hours after Anderson was born, I walked out of the NICU to change my clothes in our maternity suite. But first I stopped by the floor-to-ceiling windows overlooking a courtyard, where the unexpected New Year's Eve snow topped sharp cactus spines.

I wondered if the rare flakes were meant for us.

My life wasn't like the wedding portrait I'd cried over that day months before. It wasn't all sunshine and fields of endless green. Whose is?

Now, outside the hallway of the Tucson Medical Center NICU, I saw the portrait of our lives, our real lives, staring back at me. From the white-dusted saguaros and layered prickly pears, God's fingerprints covered it wholly. The unexpected element, the one I didn't think fit, gave the picture more depth. The image was soft and harsh and matchless. I knew our lives would not be easy, but they would become a masterpiece.

Newness abounded in the halls of Tucson Medical Center—one new life, yes, but also, a new life for me, for our family. The baby who lay in crib 5D would introduce us to things we would have never known without him. He would break down our old ways of thinking, our old ways of doing, and teach us a new way to live.

He would show me how to love.

And sometimes he would do it with a smile.

THE *Gift* OF *You*

- *Who was I then?*
  Why do I think I hid my grief or tried to skip over it as quickly as possible? If I was real with my grief, was it selective? How did these scenarios play out for me?

- *Who am I now?*
  Am I real about the dark parts of my life? If so, how? If not, how would believing the Psalms are there to show me the way to be human and in relationship with God affect me spiritually?

- *Who do I want to become?*
  How can I move forward while holding joy and grief in the same hand? How would being the most real version of myself change my life?

7

Interdependency

For two months after Anderson's first smile, I basked in the sun the way I imagine Northerners do when the final snow evaporates. There would be no more winter storms; spring flowers were here to stay, and I was looking on the sunny side of everything Down syndrome. I minimized Anderson's disability and focused on his ability. I was beginning to see the magic embedded in his extra chromosome, and I allowed myself to focus only on its shiny spindles.

I beat a few sayings in the Down syndrome community like a drum:

"He just happens to have Down syndrome."

"There's nothing down about Down syndrome."

"He's more alike than different." (I did not yet understand that his disability is intricately tied to his identity.)

I was singing victory to victory, and I wanted family members, Anderson's therapists, and my blog readers to join the choir. But there was a hole in the hymnal—a 2-millimeter hole.

The day Anderson was born, the on-call cardiologist ordered an echocardiogram of his heart, and I felt awkward as he sat at my bedside while I was in my disheveled postpartum state. Dr. Ben Burton[1] was nice-looking in a nerdy sort of way, but there was a kindness in his tone. It was somehow even soothing as he explained the pencil-and-paper drawing he'd made of Anderson's heart. He showed me the two ventricles and where he'd found a hole in between them—a ventricular septal defect. "It's so small, I'm 95 percent sure it will close on its own," he said.

I believed him.

We'd spoken the language of chances from the first twenty-week ultrasound. I had a 0.1 percent chance of conceiving a child with Down syndrome at my age, the ultrasound markers indicated a 3 percent chance of Anderson having trisomy 21, and the blood screen said he had a 99.9 percent chance of having Down syndrome. But we were on the other side of the winter now, and we felt safe with 95 percent. We'd been through so much. God would surely spare us all this.

However, what Dr. Burton originally measured as a 2-millimeter hole became a 4-millimeter hole. The chance it would close on its own went from 95 percent to 80 percent, then to 5 percent. The cardiologist concluded Anderson's four-month checkup by saying he was going to contact the surgery team in Phoenix to ask their opinion on open-heart surgery.

I didn't bother asking what the chances were. Even though my perspective about Down syndrome was shifting, I couldn't help but feel tired of the numbers game we always seemed to be losing. I walked out of the office in a daze. The sun I'd been soaking in was too bright. I wanted to hide my eyes from the uncertainty it magnified.

A few days later I was turning in to the grocery store parking lot when an unknown number popped up on my phone. "Hi, it's Dr. Burton. So I spoke with the surgery team in Phoenix, and everyone agrees Anderson needs open-heart surgery. I scheduled you a consult early next week."

I was so used to getting unwanted news that I should have known what would happen next. I was calm, stoic, and I collected my groceries as if a bomb hadn't just detonated. *Do I want deli-cut prosciutto or this pre-cut? I'll get more for the same price if I get deli-cut.*

Then, *Jill, this isn't normal. Grab the pre-cut and go home.*

The tears started falling around two hours later. I sent a fiery theological-based email to Pastor Dan. More tears. I wrote. I broke the news to family and friends before heating up the closest comfort food I could find.

And then I collapsed.

I lay on the floor, feeling the weight of God's no answers crushing me as every emotion bled out. Two unwanted moves, a life-changing diagnosis, and open-heart surgery in less than a year's time. I was sad for us like I was the months before, but this time fear for Anderson was at the heart of my devastation. Before, I couldn't imagine my life with him. Now I couldn't imagine my life without him.

What if we lose him? What if we lose him? The fear played over and over as life somehow kept going on around me.

I held Anderson's four-month-old body against my chest that afternoon, lightly rubbing his soft head as the tears continued to flow. He had no idea what was coming, but I did. Imagining the physical pain he'd go through was unbearable. And I was sure watching him go through it would cause me more emotional pain than I'd ever faced in my lifetime.

The snow unexpectedly returned, killing the spring blossoms. I slipped into the darkness once more. I realized a sobering truth of what it means to be human—the once brokenhearted are not immune from their hearts being broken again.

A few days later, we buckled Anderson into his car seat and made the two-hour drive to meet the pediatric heart surgeon. I had dressed him in his best outfit, and I was in mine. As Andy and I rode in silence between the dry and unrelenting desert landscape connecting Tucson and Phoenix, in my head I played out the conversation about to take place.

I'd been preparing for days. I'd read articles about the best hospitals and joined heart groups on social media, and now I was armed with a pen and notebook. I was not going to let this surgeon cut open my son's chest just because he was the closest option. I had my eyes on Boston Children's Hospital, and I would not hesitate to book a cross-country consultation if this guy didn't measure up.

We pulled into Phoenix Children's Hospital and got out of the car. The hot desert air hit both my skin and my gut. The moment was no longer an imaginary scene. It was here. And it felt like blistering abandonment.

I looked at Anderson in his carrier. He was asleep, and the outline of his face was so perfect as he gently breathed in and out. I could have cried. But I didn't. As I walked into the hospital, I took my mom hat off and put my journalist hat on.

"Have you ever lost a baby from this heart surgery?" I asked the surgeon. I didn't care if I was blunt.

Dr. Matthew Newport[2] looked like you may expect a surgeon who rarely leaves the hospital to look. He wore a white coat over his pleated khakis and a faded button-down shirt. He was thin and needed a haircut, and despite living in Phoenix, it appeared it had been years since he'd spent any significant amount of time in the sun. Yet there was something about him I didn't expect from a surgeon—he was gentle.

He looked down and said, "Yes." One little girl among thousands had also had Down syndrome. She went home and died in her sleep. Even though it happened a decade ago, I could tell it still pained him. That's when we knew I wouldn't be booking a flight to Boston. He was the one.

We scheduled surgery for the first available date.

It was four in the morning the Sunday before Anderson's Thursday surgery. Andy and I had decided to go out on a date the night before, and I was sound asleep from my two glasses of wine.

But then I heard it. At this point, it was unfamiliar—an angry cry from our baby boy. Scooping up Anderson's now ten-pound frame, I spent nearly an hour marveling at his face, savoring his pouty lips and puffy cheeks as I rocked him back and forth.

In the days leading up to the surgery, mundane left our lives. Everything felt . . . more. The good moments all seemed memory-worthy; the bad moments were excruciating. The reality was I felt as if I would vomit whenever I thought about pacing the surgery waiting room for four hours. I thought the emotional suffering we'd experienced in the last year would seem almost juvenile in the coming days.

With the looming reality as a backdrop, the good somehow shined brighter than normal. I cherished things I was too busy to notice, like the way Violet's little legs still had traces of baby rolls. The way she begged me to go swimming, which was once exhausting but now endearing. "Les go see wah-er."

I found myself snapping more photos of Anderson and his sister together. They had just begun interacting. Violet was finally interested in the still-new little person in our home. Anderson thought Violet was the most fascinating person he'd ever laid eyes on. Love was growing.

I wanted to remember. Remembering had a sudden urgency to it. Just in case.

I knew what the chances said—that Anderson would be fine after surgery. But I didn't trust chances anymore. I didn't trust everything would work out even though I believed it would. I knew the truth about this life, one we say often but can rarely let the reality seep into our bones for fear we might break: None of us know what tomorrow will bring.

So the night before we left for Anderson's surgery, I snuck back into his room. I broke our own rules and rocked him back and forth once more.

Andy's parents had flown in to watch Violet for a week so we could stay with Anderson in Phoenix. The car was packed, and I wondered what Andy was doing.

I found him in Anderson's room, cradling our baby boy, weeping.

"I hate this," he said. I wrapped my arms around him and squeezed him with all my might.

Andy and I had already walked through hell together. We'd held each other through long periods of waiting, stretches of doubt, and the everyday darkness. We were equally grieved during portions of the ten months that had passed between that first ultrasound and this day before the open-heart surgery. But for the most part, we handled our grief opposite from each other. I respected that he wanted to talk very little, and he respected that I wanted to talk very much.

We somehow met halfway. I gave Andy his space, but when I felt I would burst, he listened and processed with me. When I was having a day when I could barely put one foot in front of the other, he made my steps lighter even though he was also suffering. He would find an ounce of hope and shine it brightly so I could see it, and I did the same for him.

For the most part, Andy put my grief over his own, and I did the same for him. We were each broken but somehow able to see each other more clearly through the cracks. With the separation from family and in the absence of friends, we were all we had. We felt deeply grieved not only for ourselves but for the other.

There's so much mystery in suffering. I know better now than to try to paint a silver lining around the hurts of this world. But sometimes one appears anyway. The external forces could have torn us apart; instead, we had never been more fused together. We thought when we left hell's lonesome gates, we would never have to return. And there we were, about to walk through them again.

It was my turn to carry Andy, so I said what we often say in life's unthinkable moments—"We'll get through this." I didn't know how the circumstances would unfold, but I was certain our love would withstand.

The morning of the surgery, we walked from the Ronald McDonald House at the back of the hospital's property to check in. I wore jeans and a comfortable button-down shirt. I'd hung up my armor.

Anderson was in his gray air force pajamas. I held him tightly across my chest and felt surprisingly light. It was as if someone were walking my steps for me on what should have been an impossible hike. When we don't know how we'll make it through the most difficult of circumstances, our lungs still manage to take in air, and our legs carry us one step at a time. We somehow keep going even though our minds are unable to process how. Sometimes, when we're at our lowest, God's grace shines brightest.

But then the moment came. In the pre-pre-op room, the weight of handing over my baby—the baby who had torn me apart and was putting me back together better than I was—hit me. I found myself in the thin veil between this world and another.

That veil, always present, becomes even clearer in pre-op. This tiny box of a room with nothing but an exam table, a counter, and a sink could be the last place I saw my son's smile

Sometimes, when we're at our lowest, God's grace shines brightest.

this side of heaven. A tear left my eye as the magnitude of this beautiful and cruel human experience revealed itself.

Dr. Newport was about to cut open my son's chest, yet he still found me a box of tissues before we parted ways. I was disappointed God wasn't sparing Anderson of this. I wanted a divine miracle more than I wanted anything. But there, in the veil, I was reminded miracles are by definition few and far between. When I looked over Scripture in the days leading up to this moment, I realized God mostly uses people to do His work. He uses people willing to say yes to the call to bring restoration to the hurting. God's highest desire is for us to belong to Him by belonging to one another.

I put my hope there.

God was using Dr. Newport to heal our son.

It was time to let go.

The Gift

In the early 1950s, loggers began practicing clearcutting. Clearcutting involved wiping the forests of their diversity, stripping underbrush, and planting one kind of tree evenly spaced.[3] The belief was the newly planted trees would thrive without competition from other tree species and plants. Instead, the trees in clear-cut spaces became more vulnerable to disease than trees in forests of old.

For a 2020 *New York Times Magazine* piece titled "The Social Life of Forests," Ferris Jabr interviewed forestry scientist Suzanne Simard.[4] While Simard was in grad school and clearcutting was common practice, she noticed that up to 10 percent of newly planted Douglas fir were likely to get sick and die whenever a nearby tree of a different species was removed.

The planted trees had plenty of space, and they received more sunlight and water than trees in the naturally denser forests. She wanted to know why these trees had become so fragile. Now a professor of forest ecology at the University of British Columbia, Simard has studied the forest for nearly three decades and found a surprising truth—the trees of the forest live interdependent lives.

She found that through mycorrhizal networks, fungal threads in the soil link nearly every tree in the woods. Carbon, water, and nutrients can pass from tree to tree through these underground circuits. These life-giving resources tend to flow from the oldest and biggest trees to the youngest and smallest trees. She even found that the trees alert each other to danger.[5] And in some cases, if a tree is on the brink of death, it gives a share of its carbon to neighboring trees.

Foresters once thought of trees as solitary entities that competed for space, sunlight, and water. Simard and her peers discovered the truth: The trees need each other. They do not stand alone; they are a part of a deeply connected society.[6]

I believe God speaks to us in various ways. Sometimes we hear the Divine's message through the Bible. Sometimes we feel the message by sitting in the presence of a grand mountain range or at the foot of the beating ocean. And sometimes we have to look a little closer, dig a little deeper.

Evangelical Christianity sometimes has us believe that we can have science or God but not both. But what if it's not only the pastors and poets who lead us to recognize His ways but also those who spend their time in labs putting His tiniest creations under a microscope? Scientists study how the world came to be, how it continues to be, and what it all means for us.

In Hebrews 4:12, the writer tells us the Word is "alive and active." So is the forest. God's creations speak of His intended design. We are not meant to live independent lives but inter-dependent ones. We need one another not only to survive but to transform into the fullness of who we're meant to become.

If Anderson had been born in the 1980s, his life expectancy would have been around twenty-five years. Now, as this book is published, it's in the sixties.[7] Around half of children born with Down syndrome have congenital heart defects. Some defects heal on their own; others do not. Part of the reason adults with Down syndrome are living longer is the halt of inhumane institutionalization.[8] Another reason is advances in medicine and treatments, like open-heart surgery. Anderson and others like him are living longer in part because of people like Dr. Newport—people who say yes to the call.

Pediatric heart surgeons go to four years of undergraduate school, to four years of medical school, and through multiple internships, years of residency, and fellowships. They spend about two decades of their lives sacrificing and learning to perform miracles. Because most of the time, miracles come from ordinary people called to do extraor-dinary things. We are meant to say yes to this call not to elevate our own status but to elevate the quality of life for those around us. Or perhaps to

Most of the time, miracles come from ordinary people called to do extraordinary things.

save life. Or like the trees, to give away our possessions with our dying breaths.

I prayed for a miracle for Anderson, and it turns out we got one.

When God wanted to start the Israelite nation, He sent a man to build it. When He wanted to rescue the Israelites from slavery, He sent a man to deliver them. When He wanted to spread the news of Jesus, He sent men and women to build the church.

I believe God designed us in such a way to be each other's miracle workers on this side of heaven. Like the forest, we are meant to give life and receive life. We aren't meant to go at it alone. The forest needs diversity, and so do we. We need the gifts from all kinds of people to live as God intended—together.

When the unexpected hits us, we can be tempted to isolate. When we first received Anderson's Down syndrome diagnosis, I cut everyone out of my life. I couldn't bear to take their calls. I didn't want their sympathy, nor could I handle their positivity. I didn't believe their love because I had nothing left to give. Therefore, I thought I was now unlovable. I sank into a hole so deep, only giving entrance access to Andy and my mom.

Mom sometimes sent down a message from those aboveground, my siblings and close friends who wanted to show their concern. But I wasn't strong enough to send any messages back. It wasn't fair to those who loved me, and yet I couldn't think about fairness. I couldn't think about how others were processing the news for me, apart from me. I thought only of myself.

But this is not the way to live. The medical team that stitched Anderson's heart back together are miracle workers. So, too, are the friends and family who bring meals, send coffee gift cards, and don't ask how they can help but just start helping.

Maybe you don't feel God right now. But perhaps He is texting you or knocking at your door, saying, *I'm here*. We have to let God be present in our lives through the presence of others. We have to allow the other trees of the forest to give us their life-giving nutrients.

Independency is a Western fallacy. We were never meant to be single entities who have all the pieces we need to survive, let alone thrive. We are to let God work through us and let Him work through others so we can live in the interconnected community He so desires. Yes, we're to see His miracles through those times of complete divine intervention but also through the hands of others He loves. And eventually, through our own hands too.

I felt so abandoned during this time. I could not feel God when I heard Anderson needed surgery. But looking back, I can see how He was there. I see how He was the peace I found in Dr. Newport. And He was helping my marriage flourish in the darkest of circumstances. He was helping Andy and me carry each other. He was using others to carry us. And when the time came, He carried me all on His own. Not through other people, not even through my husband. It was just Him and me, sitting together on a plastic-covered couch on the hospital's fifth floor.

I had envisioned what it would be like when they took Anderson back, and I thought that's when I would break. But I didn't. I thought I would sob when they rolled him away. But the tears didn't come. I thought the four-hour surgery would entail the longest and most excruciating minutes of my life. But they weren't.

The strength was not my own. His power carried my weakness.[9] Fear and isolation left the building, and their absence made room for peace. For the first time in my life, I felt what it was like to just be held by my creator. I'd brought a book, a journal, and a Bible to pass the time while medical teams cut into my son's chest and repaired what was broken, but I never opened any of them. I rested my arms across my rib cage as my breath made the buttons on my oxford shirt pucker and sink. I sat in the corner of that couch, staring out the window over the desert city beyond.

It was bright. There was a glow. I was on earth, I know, and yet somewhere else. It wasn't the hell I expected it to be.

For hours, I rested in the unexplainable comfort that cloaked me. I only paused to give family and readers surgery updates, as there were people all over the country praying for Anderson and for us. I was covered.

God did not rescue us, but He was with us. I felt Him more in that fifth-floor waiting room than I ever had. God was carrying Anderson through Dr. Newport and the medical team. His people were carrying us through their prayers. And God delivered. He held me with a peace that transcends knowing. This is what it means to live out the interdependent life He designed, and it's necessary to transform into the people He wants us to be.

After the hours of waiting, we walked back to the Cardiac Intensive Care Unit and saw our tiny boy asleep and hooked up to dozens of wires with corresponding machines, ringing like a well-conducted symphony. Dr. Newport explained that despite the dozens of ultrasounds performed on Anderson's heart, the hole was not 4 millimeters; it was 9 millimeters, more than twice the size it measured before surgery. And there was not one hole but two. Still, the surgery had taken only the four hours planned, no more.

I listened, stunned, my gaze shifting from Dr. Newport to the thick vertical bandage on my boy's chest that moved up and down, up and down.

There in a hospital bed, my son's heart was now whole, and perhaps for the first time ever, so was mine.

THE *Gift* OF *You*

* *Who was I then?*
  How did I respond to others wanting to step in and help when the unexpected hit?

* *Who am I now?*
  This chapter is very much about how God most often works through others. What is my response to that and why?

* *Who do I want to become?*
  How can I be someone who lives the interdependent life God intends? How can I step in for others? How can I let them step in for me?

8

A Broadened Perspective

Less than a century ago, most astronomers assumed the Milky Way was the only galaxy in the universe. As telescopes became more sophisticated, astronomers realized the truth: The heavens are filled with countless galaxies, each containing billions of stars. It didn't change the fact that those galaxies were always there, but it changed the way we view the universe forever.

A disability advocate used the galaxy metaphor while instructing a class I never pictured myself taking—Partners in Policymaking. Partners is known as the gold standard advocacy class among disability advocates. A month after Anderson turned one, I drove more than two hours up to Phoenix once a month, for six months, to receive this education I never knew I needed.

We had homework to complete before we arrived. I rocked in my grandmother's hand-me-down recliner, reading from my laptop while peering over at Anderson as he crawled around our fluffy tan rug like an army man. He went from toy to toy, rolling or dragging his lower half to reach the object he desired. While I watched him work so hard, while I watched him enjoy his life, his home, I read through the history of how able-bodied people have treated disabled people throughout time.

I read Aristotle's encouragement to kill infants with disabilities. Then I read about how the powers that be in the Middle Ages used "idiot cages"[1] to mock people like my son. More recently was the popularization of institutionalizing people with disabilities.

Separating disabled babies from their parents at birth ultimately set the stage for eugenics. Hitler murdered more than 270,000 people with disabilities, believing disabilities could and should be eradicated throughout the world.[2]

I had tears in my eyes. Anderson looked up and gave me a smile while his fingers grasped a tiny book. I kept going.

In that first Partners class, we watched Geraldo Rivera's 1972 report exposing Staten Island's Willowbrook, an institution for the mentally disabled.[3] It showed the horrid conditions in which the residents lived. The facilities were unsanitary, the residents were sometimes unclothed, much of the staff was abusive, and researchers used the residents to conduct unethical studies. Rivera's report was what finally began dissolving institutions.

As I sat there in the Drury Inn and Suites Conference Room A, surrounded by strangers who would later become friends, I couldn't help but wonder what I would have done had I given birth to Anderson a mere fifty years earlier. It's likely that doctors would have suggested I send him to an institution to live.

Would I have gone through with it? Or would I have fought for him? Would I have hidden him inside my house as many parents did because the stigmatization from society would have been too great? Or would I have been a trailblazer like the parents who formed The Arc in the fifties? They refused to hide their children, wanted more for them, and made it happen through community and federal activism.[4]

I didn't know.

The class instructor followed his universe metaphor with this: "People abort children with Down syndrome because we still view people with Down syndrome by the things they *can't* do, not by what they *can* do." Gut check. We may not have terminated my pregnancy, but my immense grief was directly tied to what I believed Anderson would never do. There, sitting in my plastic chair, both heartbroken over the past and confronted by the reality still in need of repair, I realized I needed a better telescope. I had work to do in how I viewed disability, identity, and our common humanity.

That's when I caught a glimpse of Dr. Gabrielle Ficchi.

Everyone noticed Gaby. She was younger than all of us, with a petite frame and flowing dark hair that graced her waist. And she used a wheelchair. Gabrielle has her PhD in rehabilitation and mental health and runs a clinic to provide therapy and consultation services for people with disabilities. Her own diagnosis of cerebral palsy inspired her career path as well as her multiple advocacy efforts. Cerebral palsy has a wide range of associated medical issues. For Gabrielle, it affects both her legs and her left arm.

I met with her months after our Partners in Policymaking course ended. I got out of my mom clothes and slipped into something that resembled my former self, with my familiar accessories—a notepad and pen. I was there to interview her, but for myself, not a TV audience. I needed to learn from disabled people like Gaby in order to replace my current telescope with a more advanced one, to go beyond the galaxy I knew, to broaden my view.

I asked her what she wanted people who look at her and feel pity—or think that if given the option, she would want her disability to be taken away—to know.

"Disability is seen as a disadvantage. Period," she said. "But this is who I am. Asking me if I would want to be healed is like asking a black person if they want to change their skin to white. They would say no. This is what makes me, me. It's afforded me so many opportunities I wouldn't have had otherwise. This idea of healing perpetuates the idea that something needs to be fixed. Disability is seen as a thing you have instead of being seen as part of who you are."

As a mother of a disabled child who wanted to join hands with those with disabilities and advocate alongside them to make their lives better, that changed everything for me.

In his book *Far from the Tree*, Andrew Solomon breaks identity into two categories.[5] We all have vertical identities passed down from our parents, DNA, cultural norms, and sometimes religion. But oftentimes, people have inherent traits that differ from their parents. This is called a horizontal identity. Genetic mutations, physical disabilities, and intellectual disabilities are included in this group. Solomon argues those with different traits from their parents must work to acquire this piece of their identity.

Through his research, he found that parents often don't know how to deal with the horizontal identities of their children and sometimes try to erase instead of embrace the difference.

When I first received Anderson's diagnosis, I was an eraser. He would be "more alike than different." The world would see that, and I would see it too. Now I believe my job is not to ignore his unique differences but to get him to see that his disability is precisely what makes him, him. This horizontal identity should shape him, flow through him, so he can live in his entirety.[6]

I believe the unexpected has a similar effect on our identities. We thought we knew who we were, where we were going, what we believed, what we valued, and how the world should be.

Many of these ideas, these notions that shaped us, were passed down by our parents and family members, by our teachers and those with whom we chose to surround ourselves. They were given to us.

And then this new thing or new person has entered our life—or a thing or person has exited—shaking the bedrock of our foundation. If before we had the privilege of not knowing how fragile life is, now we do. Our lives are incredibly fragile. They always have been. We just had no way of knowing before the unexpected interrupted with its seismic force.

The quake altered pieces of us, pieces that now lie bare, and we don't know how to make them fit because there is no precedent. There is no picture atop a puzzle box we can reference. We can't take the changed pieces away even if we want to, and we can't fit them in nicely with scattered parts. A shift is required for wholeness. A shift is required to live in our entirety. A shift is required to understand that the unexpected has the ability to connect us deeper to the world around us.

A shift is required to become new.

This was Jesus's response to the Pharisees, the teachers of Jewish law, when they asked Him why His disciples didn't fast:

No one tears a piece out of a new garment to patch an old one. Otherwise, they will have torn the new garment, and the patch from the new will not match the old. And no one pours new wine into old wineskins. Otherwise, the new wine will burst the skins; the wine will run out and the wineskins will be ruined. No, new wine must be poured into new wineskins. And no one after drinking old wine wants the new, for they say, "The old is better." (Luke 5:36–39)

John the Baptist's disciples fasted. The Pharisees' disciples fasted. So how come Jesus's followers didn't? If they were so holy, why weren't they acting like the other holy people?

Jesus's response? Because He was doing something new.

Jesus did not come to add to an existing religion. He embodied a new one, one that was not defined by stringent rules but by loving justice. We can't stuff His new message into the confines of the old. He was not meant to be contained. His message is one of breaking free. He doesn't fit the old ways of thinking, the old ways of doing, the old ways of being.

He is new.

Similarly, we, having been crushed and pressed by the unexpected, have the opportunity to be made new. We can't go back to our old ways of thinking, our old ways of doing, our old ways of being. Because now we've been touched by life. Now we've experienced the hurt of the world. Now we know what it's like to live in uncertainty.

Now we're beginning to see.

We're beginning to see there is no "us and them." We are all one. We are all connected by this beautiful and difficult experience of being human. And once we know this, once we know life was never meant to be lived atop ivory towers, once we've trudged through the muck, once we've been knocked down, once we've been stripped of the things that protected us—or we at least believed they did—our eyes open wider than they once did. We see things we once may have had the privilege of ignoring. We feel things we once may have had the privilege of not feeling.

And it requires us to dig.

We must dig into the views we once held, the religion we once believed, the worldview we once lived by. If we begin to dig, I think that's precisely where we will meet God holding a mirror. And once we've met Him there, once we've seen our good and our flawed beliefs reflected back to us, He will show us how to become new.

My high school's building had two floors, and the majority of the classes were on the second floor. On the first floor was a computer lab and the cafeteria, and tucked away in the back next to the auditorium was the special education class. The only time I remember seeing students with disabilities was when I had a hall pass and happened to see them walking in single file behind their teacher and aides. The special education students would leave their classroom—to do what, I don't know—while the rest of us studied science and history.

That was it. There was us and them. Separate. I didn't know there was another way. I didn't know there was an option where my son wouldn't be tucked away from life.

Before the Education for All Handicapped Children Act (EAHCA) in 1975,[7] which has since been revised and is now known as the Individuals with Disabilities Education Act (IDEA), children with disabilities in the United States had very few rights in the public education system. In many cases, they were not educated at all or they attended separate schools. With EAHCA, children with disabilities began attending their neighborhood schools but in separate classrooms isolated from their typically developing peers—the way it was at my high school in the early 2000s. Despite more than thirty years of research consistently demonstrating favorable outcomes when disabled students are included in general education classrooms, this is still the norm.[8]

When students with disabilities are included in general education classrooms, gains are seen in both reading and math. They also score significantly higher on social assessment tests.

Inclusion is good for typically developing students as well. Vanderbilt University conducted a 2016–2017 study that found students educated alongside their disabled peers performed 15 percent higher in academic achievements than students educated without their disabled peers.[9]

People with disabilities are the largest minority group in the United States, but a 2013 study found that 78 percent of eligible adults with intellectual disabilities weren't employed.[10] Vanderbilt researcher Erik Carter spells out the problem: "Early segregation does not merely predict later segregation; it almost ensures it . . . The trajectory we establish in school is quite likely to continue after graduation."[11]

Carter also tells us, "Access to these same learning opportunities still remains elusive—despite 40 years of IDEA and 25 years of transition mandates. Only 17% of high school students with ID spend almost all of their day in general education classes alongside their peers without disabilities. For students with the most significant disabilities (on the alternate assessment), less than 3% spend most of their day in these same classrooms. And the majority—nearly 57%—spends almost all of their day in segregated classrooms or entirely different schools altogether. Preparation for the world of work so often takes place in separate and simulated contexts. Access to extracurriculars is elusive."[12]

Segregated classrooms lead to a segregated world.

My grief over Anderson's diagnosis was in part from shock and in part because of the doctor and his traumatic diagnosis speech. But it also had to do with my ignorance about people with disabilities. I thought being disabled was a problem. I thought it was a lesser way of living. I thought it was a recipe for a sad life. I thought disability needed to be fixed, and that because Down syndrome couldn't be fixed, couldn't be cured, my son's life was over before it began. Part of that's on me, and part of that is on my schooling and a society that still abides by *separate but equal.*

I tell you all this because I think it's important to dig deep into our grief over the unexpected. In the dig is where we'll discover why we believe what we believe. We can't move forward until we go back—back to the past, back to who we once were—and become brave enough to ask what made us that way.

For me, uncovering my ableism made my grief clearer. Yet the dig didn't merely highlight my past sorrow; it accentuated my present. Digging exposed who I was and who I was in the process of becoming. I once was someone who aimed to elevate myself, unknowingly living out the hierarchy taught to me inside the walls of Astronaut High. Now I was becoming someone who longed for equity for my son and others like him.

Is that in some way your story too? Did you once think you could control your destiny? Did you believe that if you worked hard enough, you could shield yourself from life's troubles—only to be touched by them anyway? And once you were touched by what is life-altering, and maybe even permanent, did you start to see how you transferred your belief of individualism onto those around you?

If they worked harder, they wouldn't be in poverty.

If everyone took better care of themselves, we wouldn't need subsidized healthcare.

Or,

Their life is different, so it must mean less and mine must mean more.

And then the quake happened. And you realized this lie you were fed and continued to feed on to hide from your own fragility was just that, a lie. We are all subject to the brokenness of this world, some more than others. The beauty of this harsh truth is this: If we are open to the pain and willing to work through it, we will receive a better telescope. It won't change the truths that have always been around us, but it will force us to see them. Because once we've experienced pain, we become more aware of the pain of others. Once we see realities outside of our own, we get the choice to go back to our old ways or to become new.

The Gift

The man's face had popped up in my feeds for years. I even started reading about him when Anderson was a baby. But then I quickly stopped. I couldn't bear it. Being attached to someone on the margins was too new for me.

I still wanted to think of my son as the exception, not as disabled as the world presumed him to be. I was on the side of "us," not "them," and I wanted him to be too. This story didn't have to do with him. It didn't have to do with me.

Only well after Anderson was born did I finally click and read the whole story.

His name was Ethan Saylor, and in January 2013, he was twenty-six years old. Like my son, he had Down syndrome. Ethan decided to stay at the movie theater past his allotted time, but he didn't have another ticket to do so nor the money with him to buy one. The theater called mall security, and moonlighting sheriff's deputies, one of them reportedly with a knee on his back, killed Ethan despite his aide's pleas to let her work with him. The medical examiner ruled his death a homicide as a result of asphyxiation.

Ethan's last words as he gasped for air were "Mommy! It hurts!"

Despite a grand jury, the three men were never charged, although five years later his family filed a civil suit against them and won.

For years I had stayed numb to this story by avoiding it. Then came the 2020 deaths of Ahmaud Arbery, Breonna Taylor, and George Floyd.

Mama, I'm through.

When I read Ethan's last words, George Floyd's last words—"Mama, I'm through"—rang in my ears like a blaring alarm. My head spun. I grabbed Anderson, turned on his favorite TV show, and just held him.

I held my boy—my beautiful, diverse, marginalized boy—for a half hour. My arms wrapped around his body so tightly that I'm not sure how he didn't ask me to let go. The closest word I can think to name what I was feeling in those moments is *despair*. I feel a lump in my throat and tears well in my eyes even as I type this more than a year later.

Ethan did not receive real justice because he was considered less-than. His life to the grand jury and the sheriff's department was not seen as worthy.

It hit me. This must be how black mothers and fathers feel every time they hear about another boy or girl, another young man or woman, who looks like their own child being killed because too many in society still view them as less-than, other, not as worthy.

I deeply regret that it took reading Ethan's final words, a man who looked like my own son, to not only see it but to feel it. By ignoring Ethan's story, I avoided my own pain, and in the process I was unable to enter the pain of my black and brown brothers and sisters as effectively as I could have.

It took reading a story about a man who looked like my child to taste the salty tears of despair. I know that taste is too familiar in so many parents' mouths. I will not forget the way it lingered on my tongue. I can't forget Ethan's final words that still randomly rush to the forefront of my mind, making me pause, making me taste, making me feel. And when they do,

I will think of him, his mother, his father, my own son, but I will also think of the black mothers and fathers who hold on to their children, praying they won't be next.

Hate crimes against several minorities have been increasing in the United States.[13] I don't have the answers to systemic ableism—or to systemic racism, for that matter. I am a learner, not a leader. But here is what I do know: I once chose to be blind, but now I choose to see.[14] Now I choose to see what I once had the privilege of overlooking. I still have so much work to do, but I see more clearly than I once did. Because the unexpected made me ache, and in doing so it has made me feel the collective ache that continues to pulse throughout this world.

Americans like to gloss over Jesus's call for justice and focus on love instead because we typically misunderstand justice. The misunderstanding comes from the Hebrew word *tsedaqah,* which is often translated to "righteousness." *Mishpat* is regularly translated to "judgment." However, *tsedaqah* means community-restoring justice, and *mishpat* means judgment that vindicates the rights of those on the margins.[15] Jesus loved by restoring those whom society had cast aside. He loved through the difficult work of justice.

I believe the unexpected helps us broaden our perspective so we can clearly see the injustices that

> **The unexpected made me ache, and in doing so it has made me feel the collective ache that continues to pulse throughout this world.**

have always been present but perhaps were once overlooked. I believe the pain, the disorientation we experience in this life, can give us the ability to connect with the Jesus of the Bible more deeply. I believe the unexpected helps us to then go out and live more as He did—with loving justice running through our veins. I believe this is how the unexpected helps us live into who Jesus dreams we have the courage to be.

Having a child with a disability has changed my politics. I used to vote for the candidate I thought was best for me. Now I try to vote for the candidate I think will do the best job of looking out for my child and his peers.

Having a child with a disability has changed my religion. I used to think those with the most power are "blessed." Now I see that the most vulnerable are the closest to the heart of God. Any good news that isn't good news for the marginalized is no good news at all.

Having a child with a disability has changed my vision. I once used my privilege to turn my eyes away from issues that didn't affect me. Now I can't look away.

I should not have needed to have a child with a disability to wake up from my privileged slumber. But sometimes the message of God becomes clearer when you see it wrapped in skin.

Of all the gifts Anderson has given me, what I appreciate the most is the new lens through which I see the world. This lens has shown me more beauty than I had ever known and more injustices than I had ever realized. My child was not sent here to teach me something. Nevertheless, he is my very best teacher, and I still have much more learning and growing ahead of me.

The unexpected event can be your teacher too.

What is it for you? An illness that exposed the injustices in the healthcare system? A death that has made you want to care for the bereaved? A job loss that has made you financially unstable and therefore able to see the injustices of our economic structures?

The unexpected has the ability to open your eyes wider than they once were. And once that's happened, I hope you feel compelled to dig. Because in that dig, you will meet God, you will meet yourself, and you will ask how you can move forward. You may find you don't necessarily want to get to higher ground but to stay in the muck with everyone else. Me-first mentalities cannot withstand the view a new telescope brings—that is, if we choose to really take it in.

My child was not sent here to teach me something. Nevertheless, he is my very best teacher. The unexpected event can be your teacher too.

I once rested in my privilege, but the unexpected made me want to become real—really involved in the injustices of the world. Do you feel them calling to you too?

I won't sugarcoat what I have to say next. This may be the hardest part of choosing to undergo the unexpected instead of overcoming it. This work is just that—work. It requires much of you, your time, and your stillness, and then it requires you to move. It may ask you to move away from your family's ideologies. It may beg you to move on from people who pour toxic words from their lips. And it *will* command you to speak up instead of staying silent. You have to be willing to be challenged again and again. This work demands your resources, your willingness to learn, and your willingness to act.

Some people in your life may not like your newness. Some won't understand how they can see you standing in the same skin and yet so very changed. But keep going. Unwrapping the person you're meant to become is not easy, but it is worth it.

Of course, you can choose to stay in your before. You can choose not to dig into your beliefs, not to start piecing together your new identity. But Jesus advises against that. Read the last part of His parable again, in Luke 5:39: "And no one after drinking old wine wants the new, for they say, 'The old is better.'"

This is a warning. If we throw our new lens away, if we don't let the crushing and pressing we experienced make us into something new but instead just try to pour ourselves back into the old wineskin that once contained us, we will become bitter.

We must dig into why we believed what we believed, and then we must let that knowledge shape our future. What do we believe now? What is important to us now? Otherwise, we'll be tempted to say the old way is better—the old way of being, the old way of seeing. We'll reject our new pieces and only long for what was, what no longer can be. And we will burst.

We must look to our unexpected circumstances as our teachers. Take the new lens, and try it on. You will see the world is bigger than you knew, more complex than you realized, and begs you to play a part in its healing.

The unexpected begs you to transform your personal pain into a collective purpose.

It invites you to become new.

THE *Gift* OF *You*

- *Who was I then?*
  Before the unexpected hit, how aware of the world's collective pain was I? Did I choose to read, listen, and engage? Or did I choose to ignore what made me feel too much? Looking back, how did that affect my worldview?

- *Who am I now?*
  How has the unexpected changed any of my views? How has the unexpected changed how I relate to those who suffer?

- *Who do I want to become?*
  What would becoming new look like for me?

Part 3

The Gift of Unexpected Purpose

Purpose is not static. Purpose is dynamic. . . . Your gifts, your talents, and abilities that are given to you by God, that remains consistent throughout your life. But how you apply that changes as you live life from one level to another.

—A. R. Bernard[1]

9

Uniquely Qualified

Daylight was just beginning to break as we drove up the mountain behind our New Mexico home. Andy, Violet, and I were making the long drive to Carlsbad Caverns National Park. We were looking to escape the many fears of the unknown, and a giant cave felt appropriate.

Andy and I knew Anderson would be born with Down syndrome, and our ignorance, our unknowing ableism, and our doctor led us to believe there was little hope. So we were putting our hope in the military—that the powers that be would move us closer to family. We waited and were distracting ourselves in the meantime.

As we made our way through the desert landscape, we turned on a sermon by Andy Stanley about just that—those in-the-meantime periods in life. The periods where whatever control you're used to having has run its course, and there's nothing left to do but wait or figure out how to move forward on a new path you never envisioned being part of your story.

The rising sun hugged the deep-green juniper and tan rocks with soft pinks and purples, easing us into the day the way she always does. But this morning I took particular notice.

I was just beginning to look for the light in what for weeks had felt only dark. There in our Toyota Highlander, with my spherical midsection hemming me in, a stack of kolaches between us, and the country road ahead of us, I was ready to see it. As we drove the twisty mountain roads, I listened to the well-known preacher explain how there is an intimate bond between those who have suffered similarly and how our pain makes us uniquely qualified to help others who will go through similar experiences.[1]

We made it to our cave, then stepped below the earth's surface and took in the natural process that began millions of years ago. Acid-enhanced water mixed with rainwater had dissolved the area's limestone, leaving behind these larger-than-life, lumpy, knobby, and spiky formations. A boy discovered the canyon when he got curious at the sight of bats flying around a hole in the ground. He paused, tied up his horse, and looked into the deep.[2] What he found was a beauty that can only come from destruction, and he found it only because he was willing to undergo the difficult and rewarding process of discovery. He was willing to see and to go farther still.

That day, we were in the deep. We walked through the winding path of imperfectly perfect formations. We were in the dark, but the message we'd heard in the car, the message we were surrounded by, was lighting the way. Purpose would be brought from this. And it would be beautiful.

I would get to experience this unexpected purpose just a few months after Anderson was born.

After Anderson began smiling and before his open-heart surgery, a college acquaintance who lived nearby reached out to see if we could meet for brunch in our new hometown of Tucson. I barely knew Allison when we both attended the University of

Georgia, but I knew her unexpected story. More than a year before Anderson was born, Allison and her husband publicly announced their first pregnancy. But it all came crashing down the next day when Allison's doctor called to say their baby had signs of trisomy 18. The doctor explained that, for many reasons, her son would likely not live.

Allison and her husband waited for the inevitable to happen. Their son, Deacon, died before he had the chance to take his first breath.

She'd reached out to me a few times during my pregnancy. Our stories were different, but we were similarly touched by what was both unexpected and permanent. Now we sat at a downtown café with our husbands next to us. I was nervous. I didn't know how conversation would flow, but somehow it did. The four of us were in an unspoken bond of unexpected parenthood.

We were about to part ways when Allison did something surprising. With my new zest for Down syndrome, I'd announced on my blog that we'd started a college fund for Anderson. She got out her checkbook and wrote out a generous donation for his savings plan. She knew we needed it.

But we didn't need the money; we needed someone to believe in our son, to believe in us as his parents, to believe our dreams for him were worth dreaming. We needed to be seen. We needed to be understood. And this couple was uniquely qualified to see and meet the deepest needs of our hearts at the time.

That same year we were able to pay it forward to a woman I'd met only online. A mutual friend introduced me to this woman, also named Allison, because while I was pregnant with a child with Down syndrome, she was pregnant with a child with spina bifida. We messaged each other throughout our pregnancies, and our chats were always laced with grief and hope and God.

Anderson's first year of medical issues was not as severe as her son's. Miles had a tracheotomy placed, underwent multiple painful surgeries, and was in and out of hospitals regularly. One day I asked for their address, and Andy and I sent these parents a check to help make a small dent in the medical bills piling up.

Allison told me her husband was in disbelief. "Why did they do this?" he asked. Her response, "Because they get it."

She was right. The details of our stories were different, but the theme was the same. They each held beauty and heartache. The shock of our diagnosis story, Anderson's NICU stay, and his open-heart surgery made us uniquely qualified to help these parents walking a difficult road alongside their child. We knew they needed to feel seen, just as the first Allison knew we needed to feel seen inside that Tucson café.

I knew this was not a full-circle moment but an infinite one. This was a pattern that would continue throughout my life and theirs. All three of us knew pain, grief, and disappointment in what we thought was certain. All three of us knew the immediate kinship that comes with experiencing the dashing of beliefs and the formation of new ones. We knew that harsh kind of beauty—the kind like the cave, which comes from unexpected destruction and the building of something new from within. We knew the purpose that can be born out of that kind of transformation. We were finding it in each other.

If you're willing to do the difficult and rewarding work of discovering purpose that can come from the unexpected, you will find it.

I'm not saying your unexpected experience happened to you for this purpose. Some things are just too painful. But if you're willing to do the difficult and rewarding work of discovering purpose that can come from the unexpected, you will find it.

In Part 1 of this book, we were like that boy who discovered a cavern that would later become a national park. We dug. Because digging into our past beliefs and getting reacquainted with the God who has only ever seen us as good and loved is necessary to feel known. Once we understood ourselves as known, we were primed for change. We allowed the unexpected to change us from within by connecting to our own pain and then the collective pain of the world, because we are good and holy as we are but aren't meant to stay there.

We were all made with the intention to grow. We were made to be transformed, and now this transformation should flow through us. I realize this is a bit of a paradox, to know ourselves as good enough within our creator but also to know we're meant for more.

The apostle James held a similar paradox of faith and good works in his hands:

> What good is it, my brothers and sisters, if someone claims to have faith but has no deeds? Can such faith save them? Suppose a brother or a sister is without clothes and daily food. If one of you says to them, "Go in peace; keep warm and well fed," but does nothing about their physical needs, what good is it? In the same way, faith by itself, if it is not accompanied by action, is dead. (James 2:14–17)

In the same way, inner transformation without outward action is empty. We are not required to act out of our faith. Yet when the message of our faith is branded on our hearts, the intimacy of being known flows through us. Similarly, once we know who we are, once we're open to being changed into who God wants us to be, the natural extension of this unexpected

159

> **We were made out of love and for love, on purpose and for purposes the unexpected can help us find.**

transformation is to ask God to set it to purposes greater than ourselves. Thank God, we are uniquely qualified to act it out. We were made out of love and for love, on purpose and for purposes the unexpected can help us find.

--------- **The Gift** ---------

After getting an early start to beat the scorching afternoon sun, he was in the middle of his seven-hour walk from Jerusalem to Jericho. But his plan was brutally interrupted. Out of nowhere, he was on his back. Strangers kicked his ribs, struck his face, and stripped him of his clothes. He was left barely breathing. He was left alone.

He was unable to speak, he was unable to move, but then he saw a priest coming. Help was here. But help didn't come. Help moved to the other side of the road. Then a second man, a Levite, another holy man of God, approached. The beaten man could only groan to get this second man's attention. But the Levite closed off his ears. He closed off his heart. He left.

The beaten man was just as wounded by the abandonment as he was by the gashes up and down his body. His frame bled out. His heart did too. If men of God would not rescue him, then hope was lost. He would die on this road. He would never make it to his destination. He would never make it home.

But then a third man approached him. He looked different from the other two men. He was a forgotten man. A despised man. An outcast man. He was not a man at the center of society but on the very far margins. He was mixed. He was a Samaritan.

Much to the beaten man's surprise, this was the man who stopped. He got low, poured oil and wine over his injured body, covering him, and bandaged his wounds. Then he hoisted him onto his own donkey and took him to an inn, paying the inn-keeper to look after him.

And he promised to come back.[3]

Jesus tells the parable of the Good Samaritan in Luke chapter 10. He is responding to a rich man's question about what he must do to inherit eternal life. Who must he care for?

The parable served as a warning to the rich man and others in the dominant culture of that day. But it also tells the story of the communion of the unseen. It tells the story of how our pain can be set to purpose in becoming uniquely qualified to help heal one another.

It was not the powerful men of society who showed mercy; it was the powerless one. The Samaritan man—a man on the margins of society because of the color of his skin, a man who knew the pain of oppression, a man who had been left on the side of many metaphorical roads—was the one who stopped. He chose to see and go deeper still. The Samaritan man bandaged the beaten man's wounds and paid for his care because he knew what it was like to be cast aside. He entered into this man's pain because he knew pain.

It was not the untouched who were qualified, willing, to help the one suffering. It was the touched. The Samaritan man who intimately knew the depth of pain was the one able to help the one being ravaged by it. Even though the beaten man was part of the dominant culture responsible for the Samaritan man's suffering, the Samaritan man was compelled to act. Because when you know pain, when you have sat with that pain, when you have let that pain shape you, it calls you to meet others in theirs.[4]

Suffering makes us uniquely qualified to help those who suffer.

Studies have shown that empathy is innate. Specific brain cells become active when someone is suffering. These "mirror neurons" reflect what others feel—making their pain visible.[5]

However, studies have also shown that there is an empathy deficit in the United States.[6] So perhaps we are hardwired to be empathetic, but empathy is a skill that also needs to be developed. Researchers at Stanford looked across seven studies and found that people who held a malleable mindset about empathy, believing empathy can be developed, showed more empathy to those in distressing situations than those who did not believe empathy can be learned.[7]

I'm suggesting the unexpected can be our greatest teacher in empathy, that through this deeper empathy we can find purpose through our circumstances.

Psychologist Jack Schafer puts it this way:

> Empathy is not possible unless we share the same or similar experiences as other people do. We cannot understand hurt until we hurt. We cannot understand disappointment until we are disappointed. We cannot understand sorrow until we feel sorrow. True empathy and understanding take place only when we have something against which we can judge the physical and emotional experiences of others.[8]

We are no longer the untouched. We are not the people who can walk by the suffering with our eyes shut. We have been touched by the unexpected. We've been transformed by the pain it caused or continues to inflict still. Like the Samaritan, we are broken open.

The question remains: Will we use this pain that has broken us open to be open to others?

Will we sit on the beginnings of our transformations, or will we let them take us deeper still?

Will we surrender to the destruction and reconstruction inside us?

Will we really become new?

We have to be willing to enter the suffering of others who have suffered similarly. We have to be willing to let others see us in our pain so we can see others in their own. In being seen and in the seeing, in the discovery and in the deep, is where we will become uniquely qualified.[9]

When you become the parent of a child with a disability, you see things you can never un-see. When you're born privileged, you can choose to shield your eyes from what's heartbreaking, challenging, or both. You can tailor news feeds to cater to your ideologies by using unfollow buttons, unsubscribing from links, and texting STOP options to screen out what makes you feel too much.

But when children's hospital hallways are one of the main places you log your step count, the screen disappears. You can't ignore what is in front of you, in your peripheral, or in your rearview, because life's injustices are all around. You are exposed.

Anderson was in and out of children's hospitals the first year of his life. Now as I write, he's six and sees several specialists only once a year and has biannual blood draws. I once intimately knew all the twists and turns of children's hospitals, and now we're infrequent visitors. Yet the images affect me just as much now as they did at first exposure.

While writing this chapter, I walked to the lab with Anderson to get his blood drawn. On the way, I saw a neurosurgeon—whose entire job is to operate on children's brains. I noticed a boy with a bald head—probably a result of cancer-killing drugs. I watched a girl sitting next to her parents—bored while a drip supplied her something her body lacked and a trach kept air flowing through her lungs. I'm thankful for where Anderson's health is, and yet I can't help but feel sad over what some of these children go through. I know we're entitled to nothing, but why the kids? Can't they get a pass? It's probably the most difficult issue in arguing a case for an all-loving, all-powerful God.

When the blood draw was done, I welcomed the fresh air outside the hospital. In the light of day, I was reminded of this: The burden of why suffering exists falls on those of us who believe in a higher power, but the burden of why goodness exists falls on those who believe in no higher power at all.

There is so much suffering in the place we'd just left, arguably some of the worst kind. But somehow goodness also abounds in those sterile hallways, where God is surprisingly present. He is in the hands of those who have dedicated their lives to giving children the chance at living their own. He is in the hearts of volunteers who spread some joy in the thick forest of chirping machines. And He is with the parents whose hearts, although cracked, are somehow simultaneously expanding.

I've watched parents pace those halls with worry in their steps but determination in their hearts. I've heard parents on the phone with insurance companies, fighting battles they're tired of but who keep marching on. I notice parents who manage their child's heavy equipment with a tired back but a strength next to none. I recognize parents with bags under their eyes but resilience in their bones. I may have pitied them before, but now I see them. My circumstances are different, but I know them. Their strength is fueled by immense love, as is mine. I used to want to separate myself from them, but not anymore. They are me, I am them.

We moms and dads of children with disabilities know the angst and the pain that can come from parenting them in a world that isn't accessible to them. We may never know the reason they must undergo health issues, and we may battle with aspects of their struggles, but purpose can come from the experiences we have alongside them in those struggles. I have found purpose not only in parenting my uniquely made child but in others who are parenting their own. When I am in the pit, other parents of kids with disabilities climb down and shine a light for me, and I try to do the same for them.

When we now drive through the metaphorical desert roads of parenting a disabled child in a non-inclusive world, I try to remember that this, too, can be set to purpose. And whatever your unexpected experience is, it can be set to purpose for you as well. Because we are uniquely qualified, we can leverage our experiences for those who will one day need a tour guide or provide a resting place to help get them through.

Again, this doesn't mean every experience is good or even God-ordained, but we can let the love of God and the love of others sink into our deepest depths. We can let our circumstances expand our empathy. We can allow the love that whispers to us in the middle of our painful parts to carry us. And when we're ready, we can use it to carry others.

Some of my friends who have children with disabilities or severe health issues have gone through experiences I've never known. And yet there's a place where we meet. We speak the same language—one with school acronyms, medical terms, and too much paperwork. We walk the same halls—the nerve-racking one leading to the IEP (Individualized Education Program) meeting at school, the narrow ones in the hospital, and the daily ones of therapy appointments. We lie in bed with the same fears—of others' low expectations, what the future holds, and *Am I doing enough?* We experience the same joys—the long-awaited accomplished milestone, the battle over a new service won, the law that's finally passed. We have the same kind of love in our hearts, one that is deep and fierce.

Even though our children may have different challenges, the paths we walk alongside them intersect at the corner of unexpected and transformed.

Along the way, we've fallen into deep ditches of surgical waiting rooms and people who disappoint us. We've experienced the roadblocks of paradigms that need shifting and heard the word *never* more than most. And yet all those experiences alongside our kids have changed us. We may fall down, but we get back up because we have children worth the climb. We hold one another's hands in those waiting rooms and join hands in the effort for change.

Our children have helped us discover a strength deep within and have also made us more tender in the process. We may alter some of our children's circumstances, but we wouldn't change who our kids are, and we thank them for showing us who we were meant to be. Parents of children with different disabilities may walk different roads, but at the corner of unexpected and transformed is where you will find us sharing communion. It often looks like a cup of coffee—or a stiff drink—a prayer, a tear, or a laugh. We have our children to thank for bringing us to this intersection only a few ever find.

This intersection is also available to you. Because as Andy Stanley said in his sermon we listened to on the way to the cave, an intimate bond forms between those who have suffered similarly. This bond makes us uniquely qualified to bring healing to one another.

I wonder what new language you will be speaking with those who have suffered similarly to you. Is it the language of an unexpected divorce and custody battles? Is it the language of the unexpected loss of a loved one and what to do when the casseroles stop coming? Is it the language of the betrayed as you wonder how on earth you can ever trust again? Whatever the language, I hope it will be honest. I hope it will be well received by someone with empathetic eyes. And I hope it will be laced with hope.

There is a communion of the unseen, but you have to be willing to walk to the intersection. When those in your life can't relate to your struggles, others out there can. Others who have a cup of life for you, asking you to drink. Others God wants to act through to feed you. He wants to act through you too. But you have to be willing to go. You can't avoid the people to whom you now belong. You have to admit you are touched and in need.

Once you arrive at the intersection with your people, I hope you will join hands and know you're all uniquely qualified to help bring healing to one another.

You have a deeper empathy than you did before.

You are open.

You are new.

And now that newness is beginning to flow through you.

And you don't want it to stop.

This is a new way of living.

This is the new way of being.

And it has brought you to a destination you never saw coming.

You meet with others at the corner of unexpected and transformed.

And it is harsh.

And it is beautiful.

And it can be full of purpose.

Come, taste and see—your creator is here in one another.

And He is good.

THE *Gift* OF *You*

- *Who was I then?*
  Did I ever believe purpose could be born out of my pain? If yes, how so? If not, why not?

- *Who am I now?*
  Are my eyes open to how my unexpected experience can lead to purpose greater than myself? What purposes am I beginning to see?

- *Who do I want to become?*
  Who am I uniquely qualified to impact?

10

An Abundant Life

Anderson took his first steps the month after he turned two. But he wasn't close to being a full-time walker, and I was tired. Tired of carrying him and tired of confining him to a stroller so he wouldn't crawl on dirty floors. I realized I had to put my germophobic tendencies aside and get walking practice in wherever we could, including at Violet's gymnastics studio. So in the short hallway peering into her classroom window, I extended my pointer fingers, Anderson wrapped his chubby hands around them to get started, and then I let go.

One step, two steps, plop. One step, two steps, three steps, plop.

Anderson's hands looked like he'd been playing with a lump of coal by the time Violet's class was over, but he was getting stronger. In between steps with him, I'd watch Violet complete a tumble and then twirl her hands in circles the way she still does when she's really excited. I was there to watch her, but Hope also caught my eye. Hope has cerebral palsy, and she participated with the girls with the help of an occupational therapist. Her mom, Carrie,[1] and I became quick friends. We spoke the same language of therapy, milestones, and advocacy.

One day she said to me, "I've heard Down syndrome is the Cadillac of disabilities."

I didn't know what to say, but I wanted to believe her. It's as if I were the one inside the gymnasium walking the balance beam. I still wanted Anderson's condition to be separate. I struggled with the word *disabled* and didn't want him to be lumped into that category. I was starting to see Down syndrome as intrinsically tied to his identity, but I didn't yet see other disabilities that way. Down syndrome was different—a disability, yes, but not a hard one. I didn't want to get down from the elevated status I'd given my child's specific disability.

Then just before Anderson turned three, we were at his pediatrician's office for the second time in a week and for the fourth time in a month. Children with Down syndrome can be more prone to upper respiratory and ear issues, and this time we were in for croup. His pediatrician noticed how often we'd been there, and he also noticed some of Anderson's extreme toddler antics and brought up his behavior.

He said, "We know you're dealing with much more than the average parent, and we're here for you."

Off the balance beam I finally fell.

For so long—after those initial exhausting months following his birth—I'd told myself Anderson's extra chromosome didn't make life much more challenging. We had therapy appointments, specialist appointments, and more sickness than I remembered with our daughter, but it wasn't anything I couldn't handle. I even balked at extra help available through the military. I didn't need it; I could do it all myself.

But once I let the difficulties bubble up, and then they all came pouring out of my eyes for Anderson's physical therapist, Charlene, to see. When I left her understanding embrace and pulled into my driveway, I told myself Down syndrome wasn't hard—parenting was. *That's all this little breakdown was.* I then furiously typed out a blog post telling my readers the same. I was so certain, and yet it was a lie.

Certainty is like that. I didn't mean to lie to my readers. It was a lie I didn't realize I was telling myself. My ego was large, and I had to feed it to keep it active. Like most egos, mine thrives on self-deception.

Now I recognize that parenting Anderson was and is undoubtedly more challenging than parenting my typically developing children. I don't stress over everything Violet and my younger son, Preston, do or don't do. Violet didn't need therapy for her development, and I don't need to take advocacy courses to learn how to fight for Preston's rights. But today I realize I lied to myself for so long because I wanted others to view us as a "normal" family.

I had only been a part of the world's dominant culture and didn't want to admit I had a son outside its boundaries. I wanted to be like everyone I'd always identified with, like my girlfriends and their families. I didn't want Anderson's extra chromosome to affect him so much, so I told myself it didn't. I thought I could *mind over matter* it and missed the *heart* of the matter.

Maybe another parent of a child with Down syndrome read that post and thought, *Why is this so hard for me and not for her? What's wrong with me?* Like all lies, the false narrative wounded both the receivers and the giver.

It's not that I hadn't heard words like the pediatrician's empathetic sentiment before, but sometimes we have to hear hard truths on repeat before the message breaks through. With time and growth, I was finally ready to hear it, and I jumped off the elevated surface on which I'd put Down syndrome. Down syndrome is a disability. Parenting a child with a disability is more difficult because it involves raising a child in a world that is not accessible and is oftentimes unaccepting of them.

My family is in many ways like my girlfriends', with only typically developing children in their broods, and in many ways it's not. For the girl who was always performing, who wore many masks and titles to fit in wherever she went, I was finally okay with not only my son being different but my family being different. My life being different too.

When I really look back at this time, when I'm being really honest with myself, I know the truth as to why I stayed on that balance beam so long. I wanted to view myself and others to view me as "blessed." *Sure, we went through adversity, but we overcame. Look how wonderful everything is now!* I wanted people to see my life and want it. I wanted people to see God's goodness shining through. But it turns out I didn't really know how God's blessings work.

The goodness of God is not merely the absence of struggle but His grace helping us through it.

⁓

Jesus does not promise a problem-free life. He promises an abundant one.[2]

Perhaps you rode through the unexpected storm and sailed the rough seas and thought nothing but sunny skies and a slight breeze awaited you. But now you've found yourself on new land, where the destination still has difficult terrain and unpredictable weather. The unexpected wasn't something you could merely ride out. It follows you still.

Sure, some goodness has come from the journey. Maybe for you it's come in the form of new relationships or old relationships renewed. Perhaps goodness has come with a more mature faith. My hope is that goodness is coming deep from within, a transformation into your truest self that the unexpected is helping you find.

But still . . .

Hard things are here too. Like severed ties, lingering side effects, more appointments than you can manage, or losses that mean no matter what goodness has accompanied them—like people who keep showing up—there's still a hole that can never be filled.

Maybe these hard things, the things you perhaps wish were not still a part of your story, have left you confused, worried, or feeling defeated because you're starting to believe you are unblessed, unchosen, unloved. But maybe you're living out what Jesus actually promises—life abundant.

The Gift

She was young and had her life ahead of her. A small-town girl, she was humble, and her heart was pure. Betrothed to a man named Joseph—a good man, a steady man—she was day-dreaming about what her distant days alongside him might look like.

Then another man came to her. Greeted her. She did not know him, but he knew her. He told her to not be afraid. But she was afraid. This person was different. Very different. He knew her on a level she did not fully know herself. He had a message for her. He told her she was favored by God. He went on to tell her that she would conceive and give birth to a son—a king. The king she and her people had been waiting on for so long.

She didn't understand. How could it be? She was not yet married. But when the messenger explained the how to her, she simply said, "I am the Lord's servant." Then as quickly as the man arrived, he left.[3]

We don't know much else about how Mary responded to the news she would have a son named Jesus who would rule a never-ending kingdom. But taking contextual clues from her ancient time period, I would have to believe the apostle Luke left out some specifics. Mary is a saint, yes, but saints are also human.

The apostle Matthew gives a little bit more of those fleshy details. Mary was young and lived in a culture where her only future, her only security, meant marrying a man. Joseph, this good sturdy man, at first planned on divorcing her quietly, ending their betrothal. Public disgrace would have ruined Mary, and he didn't want that. But he was still a man. He didn't want shame to be part of his life either.

If I had been Mary, I believe at some point between hearing the angel's news that I would be the mother of the Messiah and facing the reality of having to deliver that news to my future husband, parents, and community, I would have questioned my decision to say yes to this call.

After the angel came to Joseph, confirming Mary's story, and after the couple decided to move forward together, I wonder what she felt while making that eight- to ten-day, one-hundred-mile-long journey from Nazareth to Bethlehem for a census count on foot while nine months pregnant. Mary would not have her family by her side during one of the most important and scariest moments of her life (especially in her time)—childbirth.

If it were me, I don't know if I would have felt blessed, chosen, or favored by God. Would you?

But here's what Mary's story teaches us: We make a mistake when we assume being blessed by God means living a life of bliss.

In his book *The Journey: Walking the Road to Bethlehem*, pastor Adam Hamilton chronicles Mary's journey of becoming Jesus's mom. He writes, "God's blessings are not about ease and comfort, but rather about the joy of being a part of God's work, being used by God for God's purposes, and being accompanied by God's presence, particularly in the face of adversity."[4]

By saying yes to this call, Mary was not signing up for an easy life but one full of unexpected purpose. And we call her blessed.

But somehow, when our own lives cross over onto a difficult, uncomfortable path, even when we know this path can lead to an important destination, we have a harder time thinking of ourselves that way. Somewhere between the prosperity gospel and Americanized versions of Christianity, we started believing that being blessed by God means living lives of ease. Somehow, we started believing that if our lives aren't spent in the comfort of large houses or free from pain, we are living less-than lives. We wonder if God doesn't love us as much. We start blaming Him or blaming ourselves for our lack of blessings.

Something must be wrong.

But that's when we *get* it wrong.

What story in the Bible tells us God's blessed live untouched lives? More importantly, what about the life of Jesus—who was fully divine and fully human, who was innocent yet sentenced to death—tells us being chosen by God means living a life of comfort?

The Bible is a library of books with story after story about how life requires us to take unexpected paths we don't want to take. But right there, right in the midst of these long walks in the desert, God does not leave us. He wants to use us right here in the middle of the long, hot treks for purposes we don't yet know. This is what it means to be blessed. This is what it means to live abundantly.

But we do have to say yes to the call. We have to say yes to the whole of it. Saying yes doesn't mean we have to like the part we're in. It doesn't mean we can't grieve the parched land we find ourselves standing on. But we do so believing hope is not lost. We do so believing purpose will come out of this unexpected path we find ourselves on. We go forward believing joy will come again and that joy is somehow here on the desert floor.

It's important to remember that Mary's difficult journey alongside Jesus did not end at His birth. Little is known about the middle part of their story together, but we know the final chapters. Mary watched her son being tortured on a cross. She watched His oppressors whip Him and mock Him. She watched Him gasp for air.

But she did not leave Him. And He did not leave her.

He came back.

The day I began writing this chapter, I asked Anderson a simple question. "What did you do at school today?"

"House," he replied.

He used to tell me this every day, referring to the tiny playhouse he loved at his preschool. I was hoping to not get that answer. Most days he did play in the house, but according to the teacher's communication log, he hadn't that day.

Then his speech therapist, Valeria, arrived and greeted him with her over-enthusiastic tone, the way she always did. She brought out her toys to keep him engaged. I unbuttoned my sleeves and rolled them to just beneath my elbows to wash dishes.

"Come on, Anderson. You know this," I heard Valeria say, encouraging him. I looked out the window, feeling a familiar stress. *Do we do enough for him? Do we put too much on him?*

Anderson struggled with his session, resisting the work. Sadness crept into my bones as they finished the rough appointment.

"Bye, Vah-ya!" he shouted as he closed the door behind her, happy to see her go. I turned on *Sesame Street* and began researching goals for his next IEP meeting. I read an article saying that transitioning IEP students from preschool to kindergarten is perhaps the most crucial meeting in a child's school career. Tension built in between my shoulder blades. I took ibuprofen and kept searching as Elmo watched Anderson the rest of the afternoon.

Evening came, Andy came home, and I quickly grabbed the keys to the van and told my children "Bye." Anderson walked over, grabbed my face with his still-pudgy hands, and kissed my cheek. His warmth enveloped me.

I got in the van and drove forty-five minutes through San Antonio rush hour traffic to a local school inclusion group.

Ten adults sat around a long table, two of them leading the discussion. The group didn't look like much, but as I sat there, I saw the ripples it was making. The parents who led it didn't care about recognition; they wanted to see positive systemic change. They wanted the term *inclusion* to become obsolete because it would just be the way of the world. They envisioned a world where those with disabilities would be in the general education classroom and in the community without hesitation.

In one day of parenting a child with a disability, I felt sad, stressed, adored, inspired, and full of hope—life abundant. I was part of God's work, being used for good purposes, in the middle of adversity, fueled by love.

I have an ampersand on my mantel, added after a writer friend, Rachel Whalen, had a memorable experience.

Rachel's baby was born still, and then several weeks later, her sister-in-law gave birth to a baby boy. Rachel wrote about what happened when she saw her therapist:

> Of course, she wanted to know how I was feeling about his arrival. I replied that I was so happy that he was safely here, but I was also happy that he lived across the country, so I didn't have to see him yet.
> "And," she replied. I looked at her puzzled.
> She continued, "And. You are happy he is here, AND you are happy that you don't have to see him right now. Rachel, *you don't have to choose.*"[5]

She didn't have to choose. She could feel both these things at once. She could feel grateful for her new nephew's health *and* sad her own baby was not born healthy.

The word *and* has defined how I look at and how I speak about parenting a child with a disability. I used to be a *but* user. Parenting a child with a disability is hard, *but* it's so good! Parenting a child with a disability can be so intense, *but* sometimes I forget mine even has one! Parenting a child with a disability is challenging, *but* I'm learning so much about life. When I fell off that balance beam, my PR hat came tumbling down with it.

I don't need to justify the hard parts of my life. None of us can put this extraordinary existence into a tidy little box; life is too complex.

I don't need to justify the hard parts of my life. None of us can put this extraordinary existence into a tidy little box; life is too complex.

My truth is this: Parenting a disabled child in an inaccessible world is hard, *and* it is good. Parenting a child with a disability is the most challenging thing I have ever done *and* also the most rewarding. Parenting a child with a disability is draining, *and* it is a gift.

There's no positive spin. There's no need to justify how I feel. It is both, it is all, it is *and*. I find rest in the *and* because it's where the realness of my life alongside my child lies. Parenting a child with a disability is the most difficult thing I've ever done, *and* I wouldn't trade it. It's exhausting, *and* it's worth every effort. I'm not who I once was, *and* for that I am grateful.

Living out an unexpected life has taught me the meaning of the abundant life God promises. This life brings grief, and it also brings purpose and joy in and out, over and over. This is the life God promises.

The thing is, life is never one hundred percent. Even after the unexpected. I used to think the "next" would get me to that level of full contentment—the next milestone Anderson reached, getting over the next medical hump, or winning the next battle at school. But with each new milestone achieved or box checked—either for him or for me—comes new challenges and sometimes disappointment. And worse, heartache. I can't help but think it's supposed to be this way.

I don't believe we're meant to feel complete here on earth. Not because we have a God who is malicious but because this incompleteness keeps us longing. Only we're supposed to long for the things He longs for.

We can get caught up in trying to fill in the gaps with things that don't matter, things that will only serve to bring temporary highs, like wealth and perfection. But if we can get to this place where our incompleteness keeps us striving for what does matter, I think that's the closest we can hope to get to one hundred percent this side of heaven. If we fill the longing by saying yes to where we are called, if we fill the longing by bringing healing to this place in the way we're meant to, we realize no circumstance can ever fill in that gap.

So I've stopped thinking that if I can just get around this next part, this next medical procedure, this next IEP meeting, then I will get closer to happiness. Instead, I've started to focus on where my feet are now and how they can get me closer to purpose today.

And the answer is always the same.

It's always Him.

That's life abundant.

The opposite of difficult is easy, not good. I thought by admitting that parenting Anderson is more difficult, I would be resigning myself to a life that was less than good. I've come to realize that goodness, a good life, is like white light. But not in the traditional literary sense. Whereas black is the absence of color, white holds all colors. White holds the airy and light colors; it also holds the deep and dark ones. A good life, an abundant life, is made up of many shades.

Not all my experiences parenting a child with a disability have been bright; there have been shades of dark. But when held together, the whole is good. Grief and joy, disappointments and purpose, frustration and delight can all coexist. I no longer need to lie to myself about the darker parts. I no longer need to elevate my son's condition to know his life and mine are so complex and also so very good.

Grief and joy, disappointments and purpose, frustration and delight can all coexist.

You don't have to ignore the darker parts of your life. You don't have to walk on a balance beam, trying to separate yourself from them. You can jump down. You can get low. You can walk out of the air-conditioned gymnasium and take your bare feet to the earth outside. You can walk atop the dirt and grass and feel the realness between your toes. You can hold out your hands and let the daylight hit your fingertips with its deep and dark shades and its bright and cheerful ones. You can hold them together.

You don't have to choose. You can have your life and have it to the full.

If you're looking for perfection on the other side of the unexpected, you won't find it. But if you're looking for an abundant life—one full of challenges and heartache, one full of good purposes and hope, one that will be redeemed here and now and then ultimately on the other side—you will find it.

And you will be blessed.

THE *Gift* OF *You*

• *Who was I then?*
Before the unexpected, what did I think being "blessed" by God meant?

• *Who am I now?*
Am I able to hold hardships and joy in the same hand? Whether my answer is yes or no, why do I think that is?

• *Who do I want to become?*
To where do I feel God is calling me? What difficult and worthwhile journey is He asking me to take to participate in His good plans?

11

Unboxing Your Potential

All was quiet, and the exam room was bright. Too bright. This was where we were waiting to see what the blood test revealed, what anomaly made it positive. The same room I showed you at the beginning of this book.

Something bad was coming. Or so we thought. I knew life would never be the same. Whatever news the doctor was about to deliver concerning our unborn son, somehow life would always be a little . . . less.

But really, I sat there knowing so little. So little about myself. So little about this life. So little about the Divine who was present within me. My perception was narrow and in want. One day, it would grow. This day, however, it would shatter. This day, it began anew.

"Well, it's not good," the doctor said when he finally walked in. "Your baby has a 99 percent chance of having Down syndrome. And at this point most people want to talk about their options."

I inhaled deeply. "What are the options?"

"Option one is to terminate the pregnancy. We don't do that here, but we can send you to a clinic that does. You need to make this decision quickly because of New Mexico's laws."

"What's option two?"

"Option two is you go to term and have a doctor who handles high-risk pregnancies manage your care."

"Okay. Can you tell us what Down syndrome means for our baby's life?"

"Oh, uh . . . at worst, he'll never be able to feed himself, and at best, he'll mop the floors of a fast-food restaurant one day." He said this with a wave of his hand in the air, dismissing any room for hope.

He then followed up with that hero line I told you about. The one where he said if we didn't want to go through with a termination, we could let our son die of natural causes. The line that made me believe my son would have no life at all. The line, I didn't want to admit, that confirmed my own biases about disability. The line I would carry with me all my life. The line I would always feel guilty about. The line that would cut me. The line that would change me. The line that would fuel a purpose I would one day find.

The conversation was so traumatic that I blocked it out for days. Not until my mom reminded me more than a week later did the sting of his words come flooding back.

It took me several weeks to start realizing the doctor had dropped my son's life into a box—a small box.

Let me stop right here and tell you that if Anderson does end up working in a fast-food restaurant one day, I will be so very proud of him. Still, the doctor boxed my son in with limited possibilities based on his own outdated biases about people with disabilities. I started realizing this because I dusted off my old journalist hat and put it back on. I started researching and finding things like school inclusion and college programs for adults with disabilities. Then I went deeper and started learning about ableism, including my own, and discovered I had more in common with that doctor than I wanted to admit.

Doing the work of facing my past and my present and starting to piece together a future through a new lens was when the thick haze of grief began to dissipate. That's when I was able to start opening the box that doctor had put around my son's life.

I realized more possibilities existed than he had prescribed.

When Anderson was in the NICU, we decided to take a break and try out a new church. I immediately spotted a young man with Down syndrome. I sat us right behind him so I could shake his hand during the greeting.

The greeting came, and he shook my hand and said the quietest "Hi." I was surprised. For all the negative things the doctor might have told me about Down syndrome, everyone else had led me to believe an extra chromosome was like getting an invitation to a nonstop party. "People with Down syndrome are so happy" or "People with Down syndrome are so fun!" they said. Yet this guy didn't appear to be those things. I couldn't help but feel a little disappointed.

But then I took a closer look at him. He had on slightly outdated baggy jeans, just like his dad. He wore black and neon-green tennis shoes, just like his dad. And he was a little bit shy, just like his dad. This man wasn't a stereotype.

I realized my son wasn't either. He would be a product of my husband and me and whatever God-given traits he'd received.

And the box was opened a little bit farther.

And then I enrolled in every local disability advocacy course available.

And the box was opened a little farther.

And then on Anderson's third birthday, I once again found myself crying on the floor next to Andy. Only this time the tears were not of worry—worry that he wasn't meeting the milestones of other three-year-olds. They were not of fear—fear of what his future would be like. They were tears of gratitude—because of the love we had for him and how this love had changed us so.

Still, it would take me a bit longer to see that another box needed to be cut away—the box I'd built around my own life. It would take me a while to realize I had boxed *myself* in with limited possibilities.

I went on a pseudo job interview when Anderson was a baby. The Tucson TV station had no openings then, but the news director agreed to meet with me anyway since I was going to be living in the area.

She said, "You know, I can't give you a job right now, but I'm happy to look around in other industries for you in the meantime. What else are you interested in?"

I looked at her, confused. "If I can't have a job in news, I'll just be a stay-at-home mom."

I had boxed myself in. There was news or nothing else. The truth is, I left the station that day knowing I would never go back to news. The passion that once burned for it inside me had burned out. So I thought the only other option was to be a stay-at-home mom.

I had my website at that point, where I wrote about Anderson and the impact he was having on me and our family. It was starting to get attention when one of my former co-anchors reached out to me and said, "Jill, you have to write a book."

My immediate response was, "Yeah, right." It was much easier for me to call the blog a hobby. I didn't have to believe in myself; I just put the content out there for other people. Just as a side project. No risk attached.

And then I started to feel miserable. Because being a stay-at-home mom, although a wonderful choice for some, is not for everyone. But the blogging, and being vulnerable, and growing a following made me realize my writing abilities were more than I'd boxed them into. I could do more than write a minute-and-thirty-second package about someone else's life. I didn't have to put on a polished anchor face for my work to be recognized. I could be me. The me that was changing.

I wasn't confident enough to write a book yet, but I wanted to continue writing, and I wanted my work to somehow spread awareness about the injustices people with disabilities face. So I took a volunteer communications director position for a nonprofit and began working part-time for a public relations firm. Little by little, starting campaigns and writing press releases and articles and pitches made me believe in myself a bit more.

Eventually, I realized, *You know what? I need to go further. Not only that, but I can go further.*

I started writing the book I should have started long ago. The book I'd had in my heart for a long time. The book I laughed at my former co-anchor for telling me to write. The book you are now holding in your hands. The book I hope will open up the way you think about your unexpected circumstances, to choose to undergo them instead of overcome them. The book I hope will help you see this process of transformation as an ongoing gift. The book I hope will make you realize that the unexpected can shape you into who you're meant to become.

The view I once had of my life was not the only life possible.

I thought the way to happiness meant a husband, a TV career, and 3.5 typically developing children. I had such a narrow view of success. I had such a narrow view of the potential life God had for me. It took being hit by the unexpected to open

It took being hit by the unexpected to open up not only my worldview but the view I had of my own life.

up not only my worldview but the view I had of my own life.

I won't tell you your unexpected experience happened for some higher purpose you can't see. Again, some things are just too painful. But what I can tell you is this: You can partner with God and use this unexpected part of your life, right now or in the future, and set it to purpose.

Because now you know. Now you're doing the work. You're choosing not to skip over the hard. You're choosing not to overcome your unexpected circumstances and remain unchanged but to undergo them and be transformed.

Now you're getting back in touch with your core identity, the one God called very good from the very beginning. You know you're uniquely made and uniquely loved, and yet you know you have growing to do. Now you're deconstructing the ideas that were handed to you, examining each one. You're investigating your faith, your beliefs, your worldview. And you're awakening. You know you were made to be loved and you were made to love, and that this love has transformative powers. You were not made to only rest in this love but to act from it as it flows through your veins.

The love and sorrow you've experienced have now made you exceptionally equipped. Your ears have been opened, and they hear the collective groan of the world. The groan has been vibrating throughout the ages, yet maybe you couldn't hear its call before you were touched by the unexpected. But now you hear, now you see, now you feel, because you're becoming more real than you were before.

This groan is calling you to act. It's calling you to unbox yourself from your old ideas, your old insecurities, your old self. It's calling you to be made new. It's calling you to use this transformation you're undergoing and set it to purpose. It's calling you to live into your entirety.

Are you willing to go?

Maybe your unexpected moment was truly tragic. You don't have to call it good, but if you want to move forward, you can say this to God:

> *God, will You help me make purpose come from this? Will You help me use this unexpected experience* [this divorce, this sickness, this betrayal, this infertility, this family divide, this mistake, this depression, this loveless relationship, this trauma] *to transform me into who You dreamed me to become? Will You help me make it into something good, not only for me but for You and Your world?*

I believe He will say yes. Because He uses the unexpected to bring out purposes we've not yet dared to dream.

But we have to choose to learn and unlearn, to change and transform, to live like we're loved and not unloved. We have to choose to unbox ourselves from the confines we or others have drawn around our lives. We have to choose to say yes again and again to the lifelong work of transformation, to the lifelong work of drawing out God, who is already in us, more and more.

Because we do get a choice.

The Gift

Again, based on your own study, you can decide whether you think every story in the Bible is literal, or as author Robert Alter says in his book *The Art of Biblical Narrative*, that the Bible is a constant interweaving of factual history and purely legendary history.[1]

But when we get hung up on whether the story of Jonah is or is not true instead of reading it as a story meant to teach us about God and this life He calls us to live, we miss the point. The story of Jonah is about many things, including God's universal love and mercy. But it's also a story about missing the point.

God calls Jonah to travel to Nineveh with a message of His mercy. Nineveh was known for being an evil and violent place. Jonah doesn't think the Ninevites deserve mercy, so he tries to escape God's plan by boarding a boat and sailing away in the opposite direction. But God sends a storm, Jonah admits the storm is his fault, and the other men aboard the boat throw Jonah into the sea. God rescues Jonah by sending a large fish. Jonah repents inside this fish and thanks God for His relentless mercy. The creature then throws Jonah up on the shore of Nineveh. He goes through Nineveh calling for the people to repent—and they do.

But Jonah does not rejoice. He's angry and a tad melodramatic, praying, "I knew that you are a gracious and compassionate God, slow to anger and abounding in love, a God who relents from sending calamity. Now, LORD, take away my life, for it is better for me to die than to live" (Jonah 4:2–3).

Jonah experiences God's mercy, sees God's mercy in action, but chooses to not let it flow through him. He goes through the motions of his unexpected circumstance, but he doesn't undergo it. He remains unchanged. He boxes himself in. He boxes God in too.

I also spent years boxing God in. I left no space for the murky middle. I believed there was an answer to my many unexpected circumstances, and my ego was determined to find them. But God fills the void. He's in the planned and the unplanned. Instead of finding Him to be the God of certainty, I have found Him to be the God of surprise. He surprises us with the beauty of the unexpected, and the amount of grace He provides when the unexpected is anything but. He helps us to return to ourselves, He's in our transformations, and then He helps us move. If we let Him.

In an interview with Kate Bowler, professor and author Andrew Solomon cited a study he references often. Researchers interviewed mothers within days of their giving birth to children with various disabilities and health conditions. They asked them a simple question: "Do you expect to find meaning in this experience?" Then they went back to those families ten years later, and the children of the mothers who had said yes, they believed they would find meaning from this, were doing better on every possible clinical measure than the children of the mothers who had said no, they did not think they would find meaning from this experience.[2]

None of us are immune from being hit by the unexpected. Although the unexpected looks different for all of us, eventually we all get to choose what we're going to do with it. We all get to decide if we're going to look for meaning through it.

The unexpected can leave us feeling helpless and full of anything but choice. We didn't choose the loss, we didn't choose the abuse, we didn't choose this. But after a time of sitting in the dark, a time of experiencing the natural repercussions of the unexpected, a time of physically going through the aftermath, there will come a time of choice.

We get to choose if we'll do the internal work of facing our history, if we'll do the work of facing our beliefs, if we'll do the sacred and difficult work of transformation—or simply wish it all away. But in the work of becoming is where God breaks through from within us. He shows us who we are and who He wishes we will one day be. And who we will one day be includes how we'll use this transformation not only for the good of ourselves and for the good of our relationship with God but also for the good of His people.

But it may take time for this new purpose, this final part of your identity, to become clear. Some of you are nodding, maybe scared, but you know what you need to do next—whether it's making a career move, taking on a passion project, being more available to those around you, or volunteering your time and resources to a cause that now burns inside you.

Yet some of you aren't so sure. I wasn't sure. It took time to shed old fears so I could start walking down the path God was pointing me to. If you don't know where to start, if you don't know how to set your internal transformation to external good, start by taking a catalog of your core identity.

What are your unique traits and gifts?

What type of work, paid or unpaid, do you thrive in?

What is it about the world that now breaks your heart?

And then follow up with saying yes. Say yes to that volunteer opportunity at church, say yes to speaking at that mom group, say yes to meeting with a stranger going through a similar experience you once went through, say yes to sitting on that board. Eventually, your yes will bring clarity about how God wants you to play a part in His ongoing work of transforming the world.

I believe if you do the work, if you ask God to show you the way, you may one day say, *I would not be who I am today without the unexpected parts of my story.* That's when you'll know there's no more box. That's when you'll know you are free. Father Richard Rohr said, "The two major paths of transformation are great love and great suffering."[3] I have experienced both through the unexpected.

I used to tell other people's stories, and now I have my own to tell. There is no more box. I can now see endless possibilities for both me and my son. I won't allow myself—or anyone else—to stuff either of us inside a box ever again.

And you shouldn't allow anyone to stuff you inside a box either—especially not you.

This unexpected thing that has disappointed you, scared you, or even devastated you? Feel it. You can't skip over the hurt. I've come to learn that the way out is through. But as you work your way through, let it teach you new things about yourself and new things about the world. Allow it to make *you* new. Then one day you can use this unexpected something and let the pain you once felt over it—or maybe still do—remake you. You can use it to make a change for yourself and others.

The view you have of your life is not the only life possible. And if you let Him, God can use the unexpected parts of your story to open you up to possibilities you never imagined.

───≈───

You can let your unexpected experiences make you into a bitter person or a better person. Jonah chose the former. God tried to teach him through it, but Jonah was unwilling to listen. He was disappointed that God was not who he thought God was.

Maybe we've felt similarly. Maybe we've been disappointed that God didn't come to the rescue in the way we wanted Him to. Maybe we will never know why He didn't. But what I do know is that the story of Jonah ends with him sitting in his disappointment, unwilling to move, unwilling to change, unwilling to be an instrument of God's redemptive love.

I hope we don't make the same mistake. Because by choosing to let our unexpected experiences make us better, we start to notice things we've never noticed before. We start to see how both broken and beautiful this world is. We reach a higher level of empathy. We become more whole, more human, than we were. And we start participating in this life we get to live in a whole new way.

> I thought the pain, the unexpected element introduced into my life, meant my life was ending. Instead, I got a new beginning.

You will be softer and stronger and free. Free to move in the direction God wants you, free to try, free to make meaning come from the unexpected again and again with every step you take and every interaction you make.

I never planned for my life to turn out this way. My guess is you didn't either. Having a son with Down syndrome has changed me through and through. The unexpected has not only changed my career but has killed off the worst parts of me that needed to die and taught me how to live. It took the unexpected to ignite a new passion, a new fire, inside me. I thought the pain, the unexpected element introduced into my life, meant my life was ending. Instead, I got a new beginning.

I thank God for a life off plan.

My hope is that one day, in your own way, you will too. Maybe you won't thank God for what happened to you—and you don't have to. But perhaps you will thank Him for walking with you through the unexpected, for transforming you during it, for setting your transformation to a purpose greater than yourself, for helping you find your way out of that box that once contained you.

My hope is that one day you will thank Him for setting you free.

THE *Gift* OF *You*

- *Who was I then?*
  What box did I have around my life before or at the beginning of my unexpected experience?

- *Who am I now?*
  Am I seeing how the unexpected is opening me up to possibilities I never thought possible? How so?

- *Who do I want to become?*
  How do I want my unexpected transformation to flow through me?

12

This Life and the Next

They sit around a table, huddled under a blanket of
grief. Questions have plagued their minds ever since
that awful Friday afternoon. Why did this happen?
Was He really who He claimed to be?

How could they not question? Their teacher was tortured
and nailed to a cross to die. Some sat at His feet as He gasped
for air. But why? They saw Him do works that could only be
the act of the Divine. They heard Him breathe life back into
those who were once dead. They smelled the fish He multiplied
to feed a crowd of thousands. They touched the faces of those
He healed. They bore witness to the extraordinary at the hands
of a man who was human and yet more. Why didn't He rescue
Himself? Why didn't He rescue the nation? Wasn't that what
He came to do?

The questions banged against the walls of their minds so
loudly. But they had no answers. They ate in silence.

A stranger they had only just met was with them. He cut
through the noisy quiet. He broke bread, blessed it, and then
suddenly they knew. The stranger was no stranger at all; it was

Him. It was Him they followed. It was Him who spoke the unmatched words of wisdom. It was Him who came to give life to the full.

Then He vanished. The men had to tell the others. When they found the eleven, Jesus appeared again. "Touch me and see," He said. He was not a ghost but clothed in flesh. Yet something was different. It took the men time to recognize Him. His body was transformed, yet the marks on His hands and feet remained.[1]

I originally started writing this book with a question something like this: Did God give Anderson Down syndrome or is Down syndrome the product of a fallen world? The question then turned into, Will Anderson have Down syndrome in heaven?

I didn't find the answer in a book.

I found it at a theme park.

We walked into Morgan's Wonderland in San Antonio for the first time on a scorching South Texas summer day. The woman at the ticket counter caught my eye. She had deep-auburn hair, steel-blue eyes, and a form of skeletal dysplasia. She stood on a large box as she typed in our family's information and then asked me about Anderson. Another employee without any apparent disability walked over and joined our conversation, but I had to move on because a line was forming behind me. People with physical and cognitive disabilities and those without were waiting to get in. I breathed in deeply and then slowly exhaled. I tried to compose myself, unable to grasp why the unfolding images were stirring something inside me.

We entered the gates.

First we went to a puppet show. One mother fed her child through a tube, a child with a cognitive disability waved his hands with glee, and my child with Down syndrome tried to join the performance more than once. There were no disapproving eyes. There was only understanding, only love.

The sun's rays pierced my skin, but there was a lightness in my step. Everywhere I looked, people with disabilities and those without were laughing on rides, dancing to the music playing on the loudspeakers, resting on benches with a cold treat. Together. The light within kept shining brighter, trying to show me the truth that had been there all along.

Because that's what light does. It doesn't change its surroundings; it reveals.

We ended up at the splash pad, where we met an employee named Dean. Dean also had Down syndrome. He helped me keep an eye on my two boys—Anderson and my second-born son, Preston—as they ran from one splashing playscape to another. Dean and I chatted about his job coach, his housing, and his mom, who lived in a different town. He said, "I think your family is awesome" before high fiving both my boys and asking me to take his photo with them.

That's when the tears released.

Years before I had Anderson, those tears might have been tears of pity because I assumed those with disabilities were living less-than lives. Soon after Anderson was born, they might have been tears of worry over just how much his disability would affect his life. This day, the tears came because I saw exactly how the world should be. The world should embrace all. The world should be accessible to all. The world should be full of communities where all are seen and valued.

Chills ran up and down my arms as we neared the park exit even though the temperature neared a hundred degrees. After years of pondering, studying, and wrestling, it was as if God tapped me on the shoulder and breathed a gentle whisper to my soul—*This is it.*

And suddenly, my soul imagined it.

> *I am in a place where the trees, the sky, the ground radiate with light. It is not a dream. Instead, everything feels more real than before. The colors are more vibrant, love is palpable, and nothing but peace fills the air. I see a familiar face coming toward me. He has upward-slanted eyes, a button nose, and a smile that lights up his entire face. He is him. He is Anderson. He is home. The physical pain he experienced on earth because of his disability, like after the open-heart surgery, is gone. The emotional anguish from social oppression on earth was checked at the gate. He is fully loved and embraced for who he is by everyone now, just as he has always been loved and embraced by his creator.*
>
> *He is in paradise.*
> *And so am I.*

Jesus taught us to pray for God's will to be done on earth as it is in heaven. I believe Morgan's Wonderland not only shows us how the world should be but provides a snapshot of the one that awaits us.

I believe paradise is a place where no one feels less, where we will see disability as an integral part of who someone is instead of its being viewed as something someone has, and where we are not only welcomed but celebrated for who we fully are. I believe it is a place where exclusion is banished and the world is restored.

In Luke 14, Jesus tells a parable about a great banquet that the master of a house invites guests to attend but they all make excuses not to come. So the master tells his servant, "Go out quickly into the streets and alleys of the town and bring in the poor, the crippled, the blind and the lame" (verse 21). The master wants his house to be full. Everyone was welcome to come, taste, and see the goodness. They were invited to come just as they were.

Through that parable, I believe Jesus is instructing us how to live in the kingdom that is both here and not yet. He wants us to build bigger tables on earth because this is how it is in heaven. As disability theologian Amos Yong shares in his book *The Bible, Disability, and the Church*, at this banquet the disabled aren't welcomed because their disability has been taken away but because everyone is invited to come as their true self. [2]

Those sitting with us in our homes, our schools, our workplaces, and our churches should not merely reflect our own image but God's. God loves diversity because He created it. If we look around the different tables where we have a seat and see only those who are the same gender or the same race we are, or have the same orientation or abilities we do, we're missing not only a crucial message of Jesus but the central message of Jesus.

Jesus cured the disabled while He was on earth because it was the only way for them to live an integrated life. It was the only way they could participate in the temple. It was the only way because the walls of segregation were so vast. But here, He is showing us a better way. As it is in heaven.

We are called to not merely accept one another's differences but to need them. God gives us all strengths and weaknesses, and He creates this earthly body made up of His beloveds to depend on the other parts.

In the apostle Paul's first letter to the Corinthians, he pens, "Those parts of the body that seem to be weaker are indispensable, and the parts that we think are less honorable we treat with special honor" (1 Corinthians 12:22–23).

What we view as low, God holds high. What we label as insignificant, God calls essential. What we think is a mistake, God consecrates in purpose.

Amos Yong dubs this as Paul's theology of the weak, concluding, "People with disabilities are thus at the center rather than the margins of what it means to be the people of God."[3]

The center of God's heart is not the wealthy, powerful, or abled. Instead, what the world casts aside, God draws in. If this is the heart of God, it should be in the hearts of those who love Him. He wants us to work together, to learn together, to rejoice and suffer together. Our creator's highest desire is for us to belong to Him by belonging to one another.

I don't believe there's a need for the disabled to change in the next life, because everyone there will see them just as God always has—as pieces of Himself. The man-made barriers will be broken. We will all finally belong to one another the way our creator intends. In the next life, our hearts will no longer be swayed by the evil of comparison. We will see others and ourselves with clarity, and we will love more wholly because the darkness will be banished. Nothing will hinder God's light from shining through. We will recognize the beauty in His purposeful handiwork, no longer assuming He made some less-than designs.

Our souls will be restored.

My hope is we won't wait for this life to end to make this shift. My hope is we see Jesus's words for what they are—filled with loving justice. I pray they inspire us to tap into the wholeness of humanity instead of only the preferred sections. My hope is we fight for meaningful inclusion for all because this is His call—to bring heaven to earth, just as He did.

This is what I want my scars to show.

What do you want yours to reflect?

How do you want to make earth, here and now, resemble heaven a bit more? Because Jesus still bearing His scars tells us something about our own. They tell us this life on earth matters. Those scars define Him. They make up the essence of who Jesus was and is. Who we are here will carry into eternity. We will not be newly formed but instead transformed. Our identities are shaped by our trials and gifts and what we decide to do with it all.

Our identities are shaped by our trials and gifts and what we decide to do with it all.

Who we are won't be erased in heaven. Our hearts and bodies will no longer be crushed by the pain from our difficulties, but the evidence will somehow remain and be redeemed.

The Gift

For the first two years of Anderson's life, I treated Down syndrome as if it were a single piece of his puzzle. Now I believe Down syndrome is not one piece but in every puzzle piece that makes up who he is. Down syndrome is what makes Anderson, Anderson. Some disabilities are so closely tied to identity that to eliminate them entirely would erase the person.[4] I don't think something so essential to Anderson's life, his being, will disappear in the new world. Instead, I think he will finally feel what it means to be at the center of his creator's heart because the man-made blockages will be cleared.

Similarly, something so big, so unexpected, that rattles our innermost selves here on earth, has the potential to shape our identities if we let it. This is why we were never meant to overcome the unexpected but instead to let it seep into our deepest depths. The unexpected should illuminate who we are and who we now want to become.

It's often said we should not let our struggle define us, but I say let it. Not necessarily the event itself, but its effects. It's not the betrayal, the sickness, the loss that should define you but how you move forward with it. Because it should leave you transformed. The unexpected should strengthen and soften you. It should break you open and free. It should shatter the lens through which you view the world and replace it with a new one. The unexpected should change or fuel your life's work.

Too often, Christianity focuses only on getting to heaven instead of leaving the world a bit better than when we first entered it. *Thy kingdom come.* The unexpected can show us the way.

I don't want to skip ahead. The resurrection is the anchoring point of my faith, but Jesus came not only to give us the eternal life that awaits but this one. I don't want to focus only on the promise of Easter. I want to live in the light it brings to earth. I want Jesus's time on this planet to inform my own. I want to love abundantly, not only in feeling but in action. Having a child

It's often said we should not let our struggle define us, but I say let it. Not necessarily the event itself, but its effects.

with Down syndrome is changing those actions. I cannot remain impartial like I once did, merely reporting the details instead of getting involved. Jesus preached gentleness, but He was for those who were oppressed and against those doing the oppressing. I want to speak out against systems that discriminate against Anderson and others like him, the way the Teacher did.

Jesus's life came alive to me when the unexpected entered mine. I had no connection to the margins, I chose not to relate, and I rested in my privilege. Now parenting my child with a disability is my greatest privilege because it woke me from my comfortable slumber. God used a baby to show me what is important and what is not. He used a child to hack away at my pride and replace it with humility. He used a boy to uncurl my tight grasp around entitlement and showed me how to live with open hands. My child with a disability has chipped away my most hardened parts, has softened and strengthened me, and continues to mold me still.

Many see this child as broken, as I once did. But what the world overlooks, God does not. Through my son, God reveals Himself to me. And through the unexpected, I believe God will reveal Himself to you. You only need to look.

I wonder how the unexpected will bring more nuance to your perspective, I wonder how it will call you to make an impact, and I wonder how it will help you live into your entirety.

I wonder what your scars will show.

If I could go back to the girl who enrolled in seminary, who was certain books and professors would reveal the answers to the question *Why?* she so desired to find, I would tell her this: Whether God sets us on the path we find ourselves on matters less than how we choose to walk it.

How will we walk this unexpected path? How will we let the scenery become a part of us? How will we let it shape our scars? How will we invite God to use us here? How will we let it heal us? How will we then bring healing to others?

Because nothing goes to waste when placed in our creator's hands. Whether we face complications from disabilities or illnesses or accidents, whether we suffer from betrayal, loss, or heartbreaks, God can be seen there. I don't think God is the cause of our pain, but He is in the response. He is in the helpers, He is in the changing of hearts, and He is in the details.

I have seen God in the complex spindles of the extra 21st chromosome. I have seen Him in the surgery team that mended Anderson's heart. I have seen Him in therapists who push and care. I have seen Him in the community I would have never known without my child with a disability. I have discovered Him in the un-learning and the re-learning. I have found God in the way Anderson is able to soften the hardest of hearts, including my own.

I have walked in God's rays along the unexpected path. He catches me when I fall back into my old ways, and He is the gentle nudge I need to help me move forward along this land I never saw myself navigating.

And with a rustle of the leaves and a breeze that softly speaks to our innermost selves, I hear Him asking us along the way, *Who will you be in this life and therefore in the next?*

I feel Him revealing the way we should go the way He so often does—one step at a time.

I've come to look at each of our individual lives as a book with multiple authors. God gets a pen; the world gets another. God wrote His highest desires for you and me long ago; the world writes in challenges and sometimes heartache. But we are the coauthors of our stories. Before I thought I had control of the pages, but now I know I can write only my parts. And though God is the first author of our stories, He is also the editor. If we let Him, He guides our pens to reflect His theme. He untangles the sentences and paragraphs and weaves them into a better tale than we could have ever written on our own.

My story so far parenting a child with Down syndrome is both heavy and light, filled with real pain and real joy. It's a tale that tells of both hardships and newfound purposes. It's a story of love.

I don't know where the story will take me next, but wherever the chapters are heading, I know Anderson's story and mine are intertwined. I watch him fill the pages of his life while the pages of my own begin to change. Some sections are difficult, others joyful, the story altogether more beautiful.

The parts of my life I'm cowriting are not written by the same girl who cried on the bathroom floor, the girl with a narrow definition of the makings of a good life, the girl who was afraid of different. I am no longer the girl who once felt entitled to a smooth ride, where grabbing as much happiness as possible along the way was the point.

No, the masks that girl lived her life behind are now gone. The story from there to here is not a tidy one. It did not start at point A, stop at B, and arrive at C. This story has been jagged, filled with many mistakes and growth in spite of myself. Spiritual growth is not linear. This story has been and still is difficult and lovely. I suspect it will always be.

My child with Down syndrome shattered the worst parts of me and is bringing out the best. A good life is one of love and purpose, and God has gifted me both through my children, with an extra dose through my child with a disability.

And because it continues to scar me, ever since I met God on the bathroom floor, the unexpected will be laced throughout every page of my story. The unexpected has left me transforming, and this transformation is ongoing. Perhaps the greatest gift of the unexpected is the process, and this process does not end this side of heaven.

In his book *The Deeply Formed Life*, author and pastor Rich Villodas says, "We are not transformed from the outside in; we are transformed from the inside out. One is transformed by saying yes again and again to Christ's self-giving, poured-out, redemptive love."[5]

Transformation is God being revealed in us. Transformation is saying yes to this revelation again and again. Transformation is living into our entirety, the most divine version of ourselves

God wrote with His pen from the very beginning when He dreamed up you and me. We keep writing while knowing that whatever the world writes in, the first Author has not left. He will reveal Himself within a bit more and a bit more until the last sentence is written.

Soon after I learned the first version of this book had been rejected for publication, we went to Great Sand Dunes National Park and Preserve in Colorado. The three-hour drive from our new central Colorado home to the state's southern part felt eerily familiar. The ground was rough with cacti and spiky shrubs, making the mountains pop. The peaks were dotted with dark green and layered with rocky jewels.

I knew this land. I knew it because it had never left me.

I got out my phone and realized we were less than fifty miles from New Mexico, the site of my before-and-after moment. It was a time so ugly and so painful. A time wrought with tears. A time spent on the bathroom floor.

Back then, I couldn't see the beauty of it. I couldn't have known the transformation that was being set in motion. I couldn't have known the love that was present and the love that was coming.

And now, here I stood, nearly six years later, watching Anderson run toward the dunes. And like the ones behind our New Mexico home, they were the product of death and resurrection.

And they were beautiful.

And so was he.

Back when I was in deep grief over my son's diagnosis, I couldn't have known the fierce love I would feel for him. I couldn't have known how advocating for him would be my most tiring yet honoring pursuit. I couldn't have known the change that would happen in me.

Not all before-and-after moments are good. As I've already said, you don't have to classify the abuse, the loss, the neglect as good. I don't classify as good those other things I mentioned at the start of this book, things that happened after Anderson's birth—his open-heart surgery, a miscarriage, and the tumultuous first year with our second-born son, Preston. The unexpected may not always be good, but if we let Him, God will make and even wrangle goodness from it.

Most of the time that goodness is not external but a deep inner-working. Sometimes, good and even gorgeous things end up blooming in the harshest of landscapes. Then one day you may find yourself staring at that old desert you once thought would consume you and find yourself still breathing.

I did.

I inhaled grace and exhaled gratitude.

I found myself grateful for the fundamentalist church I grew up around.

I found myself grateful for the book rejection, which would push me to write something more true.

I found myself grateful for my time on the bathroom floor.

All because I realized I wouldn't be who I was without those painful experiences.

And I thought of you. I knew if I could make it from the bathroom floor to the desert and back again with newness running through my veins, so could you.

The unexpected once threatened me on every side with its spiky landscape. And then, on that dune, there I was. I'd returned to the site of the unexpected, and I almost longed for it because of what it gave me—a new life.

Once I thought my worth was attached to my resume. The unexpected showed me my worth is born out of love.

Once I thought hiding pain was a sign of strength. The unexpected showed me that being vulnerable about its existence is what makes me strong.

Once I thought molding myself into the world's ideals was what made me successful. The unexpected showed me success is the freedom to live into myself.

Once I thought to be blessed meant living a blissful life. The unexpected showed me that to be blessed is to say yes to the whispers of God.

Once I thought the unexpected meant my life was ending. And I found a new and better beginning.

As I gazed at my beautiful boy against that harsh and lovely mountain, tears filled my eyes, and I felt overwhelmed by what was birthed from the before-and-after. With sand below my feet and the peaks in front of me, I finally knew what I'd been searching for all along: the gift of the unexpected.

The gift is the One who made the desert and the mountains.

The gift is the One who made humans with forty-six chromosomes and with forty-seven.

The gift is the One who is in the creating and the restructuring.

The gift is the One who knows and yet is not fully knowable.

The gift is the One who plans and lets us walk in freedom.

The gift is the One who wants us to pursue and to rest in the mystery.

The gift is the One who holds us in our deaths and makes resurrection possible.

The gift is the One who helps us let go of our lives so we can find their truest form.

The gift is the only One who can breathe life into what was once dead.

The gift is the One who is transcendent and present in every creation, including me.

I pointed my face toward the mountain and found what I'd been looking for all along.

The unexpected gave me Him.

The unexpected gave me, me.

And there is no greater gift.

THE *Gift* OF *You*

Now I invite you to summarize what you've learned as a basis for your ongoing transformation.

- *Who was I before?*

- *Who am I now?*

- *Who do I want to become?*

Acknowledgments

To my husband, Andy. You are the only one who was there for it all—the doctor's office, the bathroom floor, the surgery waiting rooms, and beyond. I knew our love was special from the beginning; I just didn't know how much it would continue to grow. For years, you sat vigil with me as I navigated an unexpected career loss and an unexpected motherhood that required most of me. You listened to me as I tried to find my way through. You encouraged me as I found myself again. This transformation—and this book—would not have happened without your support. You love me with a fierce kind of love, and I couldn't be more grateful.

To my parents. Dad, thank you for turning on the news every night. Mom, thank you for making me question what I saw. I am a lifelong learner because of you both. Thank you for not only supporting me through every unexpected experience with your relentless presence but also for teaching me to never settle. This book was made possible by the lessons you instilled in me. I love you both so much, and I'm forever grateful God gave me to you.

To my siblings—Melissa, Matt, and Drew—and my bonus siblings and bonus parents. Thank you all for your support during the many unexpected events throughout my late twenties and early thirties and for your encouragement during this book process.

To my agent, Tawny Johnson. You saw something in me that I couldn't quite see in myself. Thank you for sticking with me when most would not have and for breathing life into this project when I thought it was all over. Thank you for your tenacity, guidance, and loyalty.

To my mentor, Dan Brown. We moved six times in eight years, making it difficult to establish a church home. But you have always been home to me. You introduced me to my creator and reintroduced me when the unexpected hit my life again and again. Thank you for reviewing pieces of this book and for being a pastor, a counselor, and a friend.

To every professional who has helped me become the writer I am today. Thank you to my eighth grade teacher, Brett Gadapee, for being the first one to tell me I was a writer. Thank you to my eleventh grade English teacher, Patricia Kelly, for pouring into me. Thank you to my journalism professors at the University of Georgia—Michael Castengera, David Hazinski, and Steve Smith—for turning me into a storyteller. Thank you to the professionals I met at WIS-TV and WJBF-TV, particularly Susan-Elizabeth Littlefield, Kara Gormley, Judi Gatson, Hannah Horne, and Brad Means for your guidance and helping me find my voice.

To Leslie Means, Whitney Fleming, and the team at *Her View From Home*. For years, I wrote on my own with little direction. You helped me grow as a writer, a person, and a professional. This book would not have been published without your support. Thank you.

To the team at the Down Syndrome Diagnosis Network. It was within your support group that I went from grief to hope. It was while serving on your board that you helped me go from girl to woman. You gave me clarity about my strengths, my weaknesses, and which way I needed to go. I am in awe of what you've built, and I thank you for what you've built in me.

To my friends. Mandy Jester, you were the friend who didn't have to be. Thank you for widening your circle in the loneliest and most tender part of my life and for being a sounding board for the earliest version of this book. To Ashley Brooke Chambers, thank you for telling me the truth I needed to hear when I needed to hear it—that I was supposed to write books. Thank you to Gaby Ficchi. You've helped me become the advocate I am today, and in many ways you've shaped this book. Thank you for teaching me with patience and grace.

To the advocates who made free respite care for military families with kids who have disabilities happen. Thank you. This book was largely written while using this program. Thank you in particular to our wonderful respite providers, Milinda and Rosa.

To every writer who has taken a phone call from me and helped me along the way. Thank you. Thank you especially to Amy Julia Becker, Jamie Sumner, Mikala Albertson, Jenny Albers, Elizabeth Spenner, Jennifer Thompson, Kelsey Scism, Sherry White, Linsey Driskill, Kendra Barnes, Valli Gideons, Brynn Burger, Amy Betters-Midtvedt, Whitney Ballard, Cassie Shaw, Jordan Harrell, Esther Goetz, Stevie Swift, Brittany Meng, April Henry, Mandy Harris, Sarah Lango, Kelli Bachara, and Amy Weatherly.

To my readers. This book would not have happened without you. Every like, comment, and share on social media, every opening of an email, is a piece of your time and heart given to me. I hope this book feeds you as much as you have fed me over the years.

Thank you to the entire team at Bethany House. I feel incredibly honored to partner with you all. Thank you especially to my editor and friend, Jennifer Dukes Lee. I'm so grateful we found each other. Thank you for seeing me and honoring my words.

Finally, to my children. Kids, you've all shaped me and therefore this book. Violet, you made me a mom and exude joy and grace every day. You make me want to be the best version of myself just because of who you are. Thank you.

Anderson, I hope you read this book one day and know every negative thing I felt about your disability was based on my ignorance and poor perceptions about life. I hope you forgive me for that, and I hope you know I love you for all you are and all you will become. God did not give you to me to teach me a lesson; nevertheless, you have been my greatest teacher. Thank you.

Preston, you are the glue our family needed. You've taught me much through your unexpected trials, and I hope you come to know that the scars you wear are a part of your becoming.

Family, you will always be my greatest muse and my greatest gift. Thank you.

Notes

Introduction: The Gift of Before-and-After

1. Concept from Taylor Fuerst, First United Methodist Church of Austin, "We Are Called to Listen," February 28, 2021, https://www.youtube.com/watch?v=kuCMd3-7pz4.
2. Reference to John 16:33.

Chapter 1: Breaking Open

1. Nightbirde, "God Is on the Bathroom Floor," March 9, 2021, https://www.nightbirde.co/blog/2021/9/27/god-is-on-the-bathroom-floor.
2. Brené Brown, "How to Listen to Pain." *Greater Good Magazine*, greatergood.berkeley.edu/article/item/how_to_listen_to_pain.
3. You can find several Brené Brown videos on the topic of wholehearted living and vulnerability on YouTube, and her research link is brenebrown.com/the-research/.
4. Brené Brown, *Braving the Wilderness: The Quest for True Belonging and the Courage to Stand Alone* (New York, NY: Random House, 2017), 67.
5. Concept from Brené Brown, *Daring Greatly: How the Courage to Be Vulnerable Transforms the Way We Live, Love, Parent, and Lead*, unabridged (New York, NY: Penguin Random House Audio, 2019).

Chapter 2: Inherent Worth

1. Author's dramatic interpretation of Genesis 1 and 2.
2. D. L. Mayfield, *The Myth of the American Dream: Reflections on Affluence, Autonomy, Safety, and Power* (Downers Grove, IL: InterVarsity Press, 2020), 6.
3. RJ Reinhart and Zacc Ritter, "Americans' Perceptions of Success in the U.S.," Gallup.com, October 2, 2019, news.gallup.com/opinion/gallup/266927/americans-perceptions-success.aspx.

4. Bob Smietana, "Most Churchgoers Say God Wants Them to Prosper Financially." Lifeway Research, July 31, 2018, lifewayresearch.com/2018/07 /31/most-churchgoers-say-god-wants-them-to-prosper-financially/.

5. Reinhart and Ritter, "Americans' Perceptions of Success in the U.S."

Chapter 3: Deconstruction

1. Name changed for privacy.

2. Name changed for privacy.

3. Author is unsure of the exact date.

4. Reference to John 11:35. "Jesus wept" is the shortest verse in the Bible, in most, if not all, English translations.

5. Kristin Kobes Du Mez, *Jesus and John Wayne: How White Evangelicals Corrupted a Faith and Fractured a Nation* (New York, NY: Liveright Publishing, 2020), 18.

6. C. S. Lewis, *Reflections on the Psalms* (New York, NY: Harcourt Brace, 1964), 96.

7. Miguel A. De La Torre, *Reading the Bible from the Margins* (Indianapolis, IN: Orbis Books, 2002), Kindle edition.

8. Miguel A. De La Torre, *Reading the Bible from the Margins* (Indianapolis, IN: Orbis Books, 2002), Kindle edition, location 158–159.

9. Peter Enns, *The Bible Tells Me So: Why Defending Scripture Has Made Us Unable to Read It* (New York, NY: HarperCollins, 2014), 42.

10. Enns, *The Bible Tells Me So*, 195.

11. Leslie D. Weatherhead, *The Will of God* (Nashville, TN: Abingdon Press, 1993), 12–13.

12. Idea inspired from Adam Hamilton, *Why?: Making Sense of God's Will* (Nashville, TN: Abingdon Press, 2018), 24.

Chapter 4: Uniquely Loved

1. John Goldingay, *Psalms: Psalms 90–150* (Grand Rapids, MI: Baker Academic, 2008), 626.

2. Walter Brueggemann and William H. Bellinger Jr., *Psalms*, New Cambridge Bible Commentary (Cambridge: Cambridge University Press, 2014), 27–620, doi.org/10.1017/CBO9780511811180.005.

3. Reference to Genesis 1:31.

4. Brian J. Skotko, Susan P. Levine, and Richard Goldstein, "Self-perceptions from People with Down Syndrome," PubMed Central (PMC), published online September 9, 2011, www.ncbi.nlm.nih.gov/pmc/articles/PMC3740159.

Chapter 5: Letting Go

1. Linda and Dr. Dick Buscher, "Antelope Canyon Photos: Where Water Runs Through Rocks," Livescience.com, January 6, 2020, www.livescience.com/antelope-canyon-photos.html.

2. Kate Bowler, *Everything Happens for a Reason: And Other Lies I've Loved* (New York, NY: Random House Trade Paperbacks, 2019), xv.

3. William Edgar, *Reasons of the Heart: Recovering Christian Persuasion* (Phillipsburg, NJ: P&R Publishing, 2003), 103.

4. Richard J. Plantinga, Thomas R. Thompson, and Matthew D. Lundberg, *An Introduction to Christian Theology* (Cambridge, UK: Cambridge University Press, 2010).

5. This idea is paraphrased from books by author and pastor Adam Hamilton.

6. "Geology of White Sands," NPS.gov (U.S. National Park Service), www.nps.gov/whsa/learn/geology-of-white-sands.htm.

7. Sarah Bessey, *Miracles and Other Reasonable Things: A Story of Unlearning and Relearning God* (New York, NY: Howard Books, 2019), 167.

8. Reference to Ecclesiastes 3:11.

Chapter 6: Becoming Real

1. Walter Brueggemann, *Spirituality of the Psalms* (Fortress Press, 2002), Kindle locations 53–55.

2. Psalm 22:1, quoted by Jesus in Matthew 27:46.

3. Walter Brueggemann uses this phrase in *Spirituality of the Psalms* (location 61).

Chapter 7: Interdependency

1. Name changed for privacy.

2. Name changed for privacy.

3. "Research Work Finds Clearcutting the Best Method in the Douglas-Fir Region," Forest History Society, https://foresthistory.org/research-explore/us-forest-service-history/policy-and-law/forest-management/controversy-over-clearcutting/controversy-over-clearcutting-timeline/research-work-finds-clearcutting-the-best-method-in-the-douglas-fir-region/.

4. Ferris Jabr, "The Social Life of Forests," *The New York Times Magazine*, December 7, 2020, www.nytimes.com/interactive/2020/12/02/magazine/tree-communication-mycorrhiza.html.

5. Monica A. Gorzelak, Amanda K. Asay, Brian J. Pickles, and Suzanne W. Simard, "Inter-plant Communication Through Mycorrhizal Networks Mediates Complex Adaptive Behaviour in Plant Communities," May 15, 2015, PubMed Central (PMC), www.ncbi.nlm.nih.gov/pmc/articles/PMC4497361/.

6. Jabr, "The Social Life of Forests."

7. "Facts and FAQ about Down Syndrome," Global Down Syndrome Foundation, www.globaldownsyndrome.org/about-down-syndrome/facts-about-down-syndrome/.

8. "Facts and FAQ about Down Syndrome."

9. Reference to 2 Corinthians 12:9.

Chapter 8: A Broadened Perspective

1. The Minnesota Council on Developmental Disabilities captures the treatment of those with disabilities in the Ancient Era from 1500 BC–AD 475 through their Parallels in Time series.

2. Andrew Solomon, *Far from the Tree: Parents, Children and the Search for Identity* (New York, NY: Scribner, 2012), 27.

3. "The Willowbrook Case," ABC News, https://www.youtube.com/watch?v=qzNFRn5TTtc.

4. The Arc, https://thearc.org/about-us/history/.

5. Andrew Solomon, *Far from the Tree: Parents, Children and the Search for Identity* (New York, NY: Simon & Schuster, 2012), 2.

6. Based on a Twitter post by author Imani Barbarin, January 20, 2021, https://twitter.com/imani_barbarin/status/1351969285615316992?lang=en Crutches and Spice.

7. "Timeline of the Individuals with Disabilities Education Act (IDEA)," KU, The University of Kansas, educationonline.ku.edu/community/idea-timeline.

8. Equity Based Inclusion | MCIE, https://www.mcie.org/_files/ugd/34e35e_0f6d9a16276648a2b68181b800d9e3e2.pdf.

9. Patti Logsdon, Mark Samudre, and Harold Kleinert, "A Qualitative Study of the Impact of Peer Networks and Peer Support Arrangements in Project Pilot Schools," Human Development Institute, University of Kentucky, Winter 2018, www.hdi.uky.edu/wp-content/uploads/2018/01/ResearchBrief_Winter2018b.pdf.

10. John Butterworth, Frank A. Smith, Allison Cohen Hall, Alberto Migliore, Jean Winsor, Daria Domin, "The National Report on Employment Services and Outcomes," Institute for Community Inclusion (UCEDD), University of Massachusetts Boston, Winter 2013, StateData Book, book.statedata.info/13/.

11. Erik W. Carter, "What Matters Most: Toward a Future of Flourishing," TASH Connections, Vol. 41, Issue 3, Fall 2015, Grand Valley State University, https://www.gvsu.edu/cms4/asset/64CB422A-ED08-43F0-F795CA9DE364B6BE/2015_what_matters_most_tash_connections.pdf.

12. Carter, "What Matters Most," 16.

13. Christina Carrega and Priya Krishnakumar, "Hate crime reports in US surge to the highest level in 12 years," CNN, October 26, 2021, https://www.cnn.com/2021/08/30/us/fbi-report-hate-crimes-rose-2020/index.html.

14. Reference to the hymn "Amazing Grace."

15. David P. Gushee and Glen H. Stassen, *Kingdom Ethics: Following Jesus in Contemporary Context* (Grand Rapids, MI: Eerdmans, 2016), Kindle edition, 126–127.

Part 3: The Gift of Unexpected Purpose

1. A. R. Bernard, "Pastor A.R. Bernard on What You Might Not Understand About Your Purpose | SuperSoul Sunday | OWN," *Super Soul Sunday*, OWN, season 8, episode 802, https://www.youtube.com/watch?v=5KPBd7KPYxw.

Chapter 9: Uniquely Qualified

1. Andy Stanley, "In the Meantime | Comfort Zone," NPM Series Sites, September 21, 2014, series.northpointministries.org/in-the-meantime/comfort-zone.
2. Jim White, "Carlsbad Caverns National Park—Part 2," Skyline Civil Group, www.skylinecivilgroup.com/carlsbad-nm-jim-white/.
3. Author's dramatic interpretation of the parable of the Good Samaritan found in Luke 10:25–37.
4. Concept from Miguel A. De La Torre, *Reading the Bible from the Margins* (Indianapolis, IN: Orbis Books, 2002), Kindle edition.
5. Pier Francesco Ferrari and Giacomo Rizzolatti, "Mirror Neuron Research: The Past and the Future," National Library of Medicine, PubMed Central (PMC), June 5, 2014, www.ncbi.nlm.nih.gov/pmc/articles/PMC4006175/.
6. Sara H. Konrath, Edward H. O'Brien, and Courtney Hsing, "Changes in Dispositional Empathy in American College Students Over Time: A Meta-Analysis," SAGE Journals, August 5, 2010, journals.sagepub.com/doi/abs/10.1177/1088868310377395.
7. Karina Schumann, J. Zaki, and C. Dweck, "Addressing the Empathy Deficit: Beliefs About the Malleability of Empathy Predict Effortful Responses when Empathy is Challenging," Semantic Scholar | AI-Powered Research Tool, August 31, 2014, www.semanticscholar.org/paper/Addressing-the-empathy-deficit:-beliefs-about-the-Schumann-Zaki/bc9b43f665b947ddf20df2fda55ecb758565c6a1.
8. Jack Schafer, "The Fruit of Pain, Hardship, and Disappointment Is Empathy," *Psychology Today*, September 27, 2018, https://www.psychologytoday.com/us/blog/let-their-words-do-the-talking/201809/the-fruit-pain-hardship-and-disappointment-is-empathy?amp.
9. Concept from Stanley, "In the Meantime | Comfort Zone."

Chapter 10: An Abundant Life

1. Name changed for privacy.
2. Reference to John 10:10.
3. Author's dramatic interpretation of Luke 1:26–38.
4. Adam Hamilton, *The Journey: Walking the Road to Bethlehem* (Nashville, TN: Abingdon Press, 2011), Kindle edition, location 758.
5. Rachel Whalen, "The Power of 'And.'" *Still Standing Magazine*, April 24, 2019, https://stillstandingmag.com/2019/04/24/the-power-of-and/.

Chapter 11: Unboxing Your Potential

1. Robert Alter, *The Art of Biblical Narrative* (New York, NY: Basic Books), 2011.
2. Kate Bowler, "Andrew Solomon: The Stories of Who We Are," podcast, July 30, 2019, https://katebowler.com/podcasts/andrew-solomon-the-stories-of-who-we-are.

3. Jen Hatmaker, "Live Yourself into a New Way of Thinking: Richard Rohr," April 9, 2019, podcast, https://jenhatmaker.com/podcast/series-16/live-yourself-into-a-new-way-of-thinking-richard-rohr.

Chapter 12: This Life and the Next

1. Author's dramatic interpretation of events recorded in Luke 24.
2. Amos Yong, *The Bible, Disability, and the Church: A New Vision of the People of God* (Grand Rapids, MI: Eerdmans, 2011), 131–133.
3. Yong, *The Bible, Disability, and the Church*, 95.
4. Concept from Yong, *The Bible, Disability, and the Church*, 121.
5. Rich Villodas, *The Deeply Formed Life* (Colorado Springs, CO: WaterBrook, 2020), xvii.

Jillian Benfield is a former television news anchor and holds a broadcast journalism degree from the University of Georgia. Jillian's essays about living an unexpected life have appeared on sites such as *TODAY*, *Good Morning America*, *Yahoo! News*, *ABC News*, and more. Jillian is a past board member of the Down Syndrome Diagnosis Network and is currently a Medical Outreach team member. She is a part of the National Down Syndrome Congress's National Down Syndrome Advocacy Coalition and is a Partners in Policymaking graduate. After living in six states in eight years with the military, Jillian and her husband, Andy, have finally settled on Florida's beautiful Space Coast with their three children.